God Of Justice

A Look At
The Ten Commandments
For The 21st Century

David E. Leininger

CSS Publishing Company, Inc., Lima, Ohio

GOD OF JUSTICE

Copyright © 2007 by
CSS Publishing Company, Inc.
Lima, Ohio

Most scripture quotations are from the Holy Bible, New International Version. Copyright
© 1973, 1978, 1984 International Bible Society. Used by permission of Zondervan Bible
Publishers. All rights reserved.

Scripture quotations marked (NRSV) are taken from the New Revised Standard Version of
the Bible, copyright 1989 by the Division of Christian Education of the National Council of
the Churches of Christ in the USA. Used by permission.

Scripture quotations marked (KJV) are taken from the King James Version of the Bible, in
the public domain.

Library of Congress Cataloging-in-Publication Data

Leininger, David E., 1944-
    God of justice : a look at the Ten commandments for the 21st century / David E.
Leininger.
        p. cm.
    ISBN 0-7880-2462-0 (perfect bound : alk. paper)
    1. Ten commandments—Textbooks. I. title.

BS1285.55.L45 2007
241.5'2—dc22

                                                                    2007024838

For more information about CSS Publishing Company resources, visit our website at
www.csspub.com or email us at csr@csspub.com or call (800) 241-4056.

Cover design by Barbara Spencer
ISBN-13: 978-0-7880-2462-7
ISBN-10: 0-7880-2462-0   PRINTED IN USA

To the wonderful friends in the congregation of
First Presbyterian Church
Warren, Pennsylvania,
people who have shown their commitment
to the principles of God's justice
in their lives and ministry

Table Of Contents

General Study Questions

1. How does our society understand the Ten Commandments?

2. How does society *mis*understand the Ten Commandments?

3. What do you think about displaying the Ten Commandments in public buildings? In a pluralistic society, what guidelines should be followed concerning any such displays? If displaying is okay, which version should it be and why?

4. If the Decalogue is primarily concerned with social justice as the author suggests, how do the commandments impact individual moral/ethical choices?

Introduction

God cares about justice! Hardly a startling statement. That has been a bedrock principle of religion for centuries. For some people, that is God's most important attribute — if you get out of line, God's gonna get you! That is justice, after all. In fact, it is precisely that kind of thinking that gives some dear hearts great comfort — an assurance that, one day, God will make everything right: "the wrong shall fail/the right prevail," the upside down will be made right side up, the good will be rewarded, and the evil will pay.

To be sure, that is contrary to the Christian tradition, even though more church members than we might care to admit cling to that hope. Church teaching is that Christians are not rewarded based on our good or our evil. Instead, we look to the cross of Jesus Christ and there see our own guilt crucified "in his body on the tree, so that we might die to sins and live for righteousness; by his wounds you have been healed" (1 Peter 2:24). God's justice has been shown to be tempered with incredible grace.

Then where are we with this insistence on a God of justice? Simply here: God cares about justice ... as well as a lot of other stuff, okay? And I, for one, am glad.

We find evidence of God's concern early on in the pages of scripture in the divine dealings with the covenant community of Israel. The most prominent statement on God's standards for justice is the Ten Commandments.

The Decalogue is often misunderstood, particularly now as it has been caught up in the "culture wars" of recent years. Most notoriously, Judge Roy Moore, of Etowah County, Alabama, was sued by the American Civil Liberties Union and the Alabama Free Thought Association in 1995 for displaying the Ten Commandments on his courtroom wall. Judge Moore's contention was that these rules formed the basis of western jurisprudence, and they would be a good reminder of where we have all come from. Moore lost that case, but used the fallout to mount a campaign for the State Supreme Court, a race that he won, which eventually led him to the lofty position of Chief Justice. From that perch, he decided to up the ante by, instead of simply posting the commandments on the wall, having them engraved on a two-and-a-half ton hunk of granite, then late one night, installing that hunk in the courthouse rotunda. Another legal challenge ensued, and this time, the judge not only lost the case, he lost his job.

Yes, the Ten Commandments are often in the news, but the sad truth is that relatively few people can say what they are. We perhaps should have known that these commandments are in trouble. If we had been listening, the irrepressible Ted Turner would have told us that. He declared them obsolete. The creator of Cable News Network told members of the National Newspaper Association in Atlanta that the Ten Commandments do not relate to current global problems, such as overpopulation and the arms race. "We're living with outmoded rules," Turner said. "The rules we're living under [are] the Ten Commandments, and I bet nobody here even pays much attention to 'em, because they are too old. When Moses went up on the mountain there were no nuclear weapons; there was no poverty. Today, the commandments wouldn't go over. Nobody around likes to be commanded. Commandments are out." So says Ted Turner.

Are they? No, they are not. And the reason they are not is that the Ten Commandments are the bedrock of justice. God did not pass these on to Moses as a way to keep us in line; rather, these words were a gracious gift to help us get along together in a healthy society.

Having said that, a good deal of misunderstanding has burdened the interpretation of the Decalogue. It starts with Ted Turner's objection stating that nobody "likes to be commanded." True enough. But if we go back to the very beginning of the text, we find God saying, "I AM the Lord your God, who brought you out of Egypt, out of the land of slavery." God does not start by giving the Israelites rules. "I AM" starts by loving them, by freeing them from slavery and getting them out of Egypt. Then and only then can this frightened and anxious people know that this God deserves to be listened to. This God is on their side and is helping them find the good life. These are not *laws* — they have no penalties attached for breaking them. In the Hebrew Bible, they are known simply as the "Ten Words" — God's words for the establishment of the kind of society in which we would all like to live. The sermons that follow are an effort to provide a contemporary understanding of God's guidelines.

I would love to say that our twenty-first-century society has taken them seriously and tried, as Judge Moore in his rather unusual way did, to use them as the basis for our life together. Sadly, we know such is not the case. In fact, it is *so* not the case that we have every right to be angry, the righteous indignation that Jesus himself felt when he saw things that ought not to be.

We can be angry that a nation which prides itself on providing "equal justice under law" provides it depending on the color of a person's skin or how much money he or she can afford to pay a legal "dream team." Remember, God cares about justice.

We can be angry about the perpetuation of a system that offers medical treatment, not on the basis of need, but on the basis of how much money someone has. The people who have no money and the people who have a lot of money get care — those in the middle may not. Remember, God cares about justice.

We can be angry about a society which allows a ready supply of deadly weapons to almost anyone with the result that, of all the technically advanced nations of the world, we have an exponentially higher murder rate than any other. Remember, God cares about justice.

We can be angry when women, though working every bit as hard as any man, still face discrimination, abuse, harassment, and unfair pay. Remember, God cares about justice.

We can be angry when white-collar criminals in corporate boardrooms pay themselves fat salaries and bonuses, looting companies into bankruptcy, and leaving workers and retirees to fend for themselves. Remember, God cares about justice.

We can be angry at national priorities that allocate hundreds of billions of dollars to defense every year, equaling the amount allocated in total by all the other nations on the face of the earth, almost 200 of them — when there are people right here in our own backyard who go without food, clothing, or medicine because they need our help to get them. Remember, God cares about justice.

— David Leininger

First Commandment

One God, Only One

Now a man came up to Jesus and asked, "Teacher, what good thing must I do to get eternal life?"

"Why do you ask me about what is good?" Jesus replied. "There is only One who is good. If you want to enter life, obey the commandments."

"Which ones?" the man inquired.

Jesus replied, "'Do not murder, do not commit adultery, do not steal, do not give false testimony, honor your father and mother,' and 'love your neighbor as yourself.'"

"All these I have kept," the young man said. "What do I still lack?"

Jesus answered, "If you want to be perfect, go, sell your possessions and give to the poor, and you will have treasure in heaven. Then come, follow me."

When the young man heard this, he went away sad, because he had great wealth. — Matthew 19:16-22

Right near the end of the last century, just prior to the turn of the millennium, someone decided to compile a list of the 100 best English-language novels of the past hundred years. It got quite a bit of comment because virtually no one agreed with the list-makers in their selections, and virtually everyone agreed that the number one pick, James Joyce's *Ulysses*, is a miserable read. Still, no one could agree on a new number one, nor, for that matter, any substitute list either. About all anyone would grant is that Americans do love lists. Ask David Letterman. Or David Wallechinsky who wrote something called *The Book of Lists* or Geoff Tiballs who wrote the *Best Book of Lists Ever* or Sandra Chron, author of *The All-New Book of Lists for Kids*. In fact, the *Arizona Republic* went so far as to compile a list of lists, the "50

11

Best Lists of All Time." Among the top ten are the Seven Wonders of the Ancient World, The Bill of Rights, and the FBI's Ten Most Wanted. But the consensus pick for the number one list ever was the Ten Commandments.

Good choice? Most people would agree. Certainly those who have been battling long and hard for public display of the Decalogue in courthouses and schoolrooms, and the like, would agree. In Alabama, Judge Roy Moore made a political career of that effort, first in a campaign for the State Supreme Court and, most recently, as candidate for the Republican nomination as governor. Truth be told, he needed the job because, as we news junkies know, he had been summarily fired from his Supreme Court seat after he installed a granite monument featuring the Ten Commandments in the courthouse rotunda and subsequently refused a court order to remove it. Of course, Alabama is about as Bible Belt as you can get, so you might expect that Judge Roy would do right well with the electorate with his particular issue. As it turns out, though, he lost the primary election to incumbent Bob Riley in a landslide. One might be tempted to say that the result indicates that even in Alabama they are getting tired of the culture wars, but in that same election, by a four-to-one margin, voters passed a ban on gay marriage.

So saying, the Gallup Organization has found, in its regular poll investigating the religious beliefs and practices of modern Americans, that approximately 85% of us feel that the Decalogue is still applicable for us today. But the polls show something else, too: that of the 85%, less than half can name even five of the commandments. Either churches are not doing a proper job of teaching the commandments of God, or the people are not listening. Probably some of both. Churches used to spend much more time teaching the Ten Commandments. In England, during the Reformation there was a law that required that the Lord's Prayer, the Apostles' Creed, and the Ten Commandments be prominently displayed on plaques on the wall. It was a tradition that made its way across the Atlantic as is evidenced by such plaques on the walls of America's colonial churches. The commandments were also used much more in the liturgy of worship, either preceding the Confession of Sin to call attention to the standards being violated or following the Assurance of Pardon as a guide to Christian living, but that practice faded.[1]

No doubt, you are aware that there is more than one version of the Ten Commandments. In Judge Moore's tradition, in my Reformed Tradition, in the Orthodox churches, and on some of the yard signs that we see here and there, the first commandment is "No other Gods" followed by the second commandment, "No graven images." But in the Lutheran and the Roman Catholic traditions, those two are considered as one. And good arguments can be made for either position. To come up with a list of ten, they divide what we call the final one about not coveting a neighbor's house or wife or servants and the like, into "Do not covet your neighbor's wife," number nine, and finally, "Do not covet your neighbor's house, servants, animals, or any other possession" as number ten, and they base that on the order found in the fifth chapter of Deuteronomy where we find another rendering of this Decalogue.

A brief overview is needed here. "I am the Lord your God, who brought you out of Egypt, out of the land of slavery" (Exodus 20:2). God does not start by giving the Israelites rules. "I AM" starts by loving them, by freeing them from slavery in a world where slavery was rampant and by getting them out of Egypt. This God is already on the Israelites' side and is now ready to help them find the good life. As we noted in the introduction, these are not *laws* in the strictest sense — they have no penalties attached for breaking them. In the Hebrew Bible, they are known simply as the "Ten Words" — God's words for the establishment of the kind of society in which we would all like to live.

By the way, have you ever heard that these commandments are best understood by dividing them into two tables: the first group (1-4) for dealing with God; the second (5-10) for dealing with one another? They are often taught that way. That is the way I learned them, too, and subsequently, I taught them that way. No longer. I am convinced that a better way to understand them is to realize that *all* of them are about a just society. They are not prescriptions for personal morality; they are to be understood communally and corporately. In fact, in Hebrew, God uses the unusual second person singular form of address in formulating the commands: "You [singular], Israel, shall not...." Individual behavior will follow along.

No other gods — no images — do not misuse the Lord's name — keep the sabbath — honor your father and mother — do not kill — do not steal — do not commit adultery — do not bear false witness — and do not covet the things that your neighbor counts on for a decent life. Ten commandments to define a just society. As we say, obviously not a penal code — rather, a list more akin to our Bill of Rights, the first ten amendments to our US Constitution. Yes, a full-blown legal code will be needed down the road with all the "If you do this, then you will get this," and, indeed, every one of these "policy statements," except the one about coveting, are reiterated elsewhere in the Torah in the form of law and penalty. Meanwhile, these guidelines will give your emerging society a good and just foundation.

Down to cases. The place to begin, of course, is at the beginning. Number One: Exodus 20:3 — "You shall have no other gods before me."[2] On its face, that sounds like the plaintive cry of a god who is afraid of being ignored or supplanted, like a teenage boy who is terrified that his girlfriend might dump him — a pretty wimpy god. But, remember, this is not about God; this is about *us* and a just society. More about that in a moment.

"I am to be your only God!" That seems clear enough. No problem. The Gallup polls indicate that 95% of Americans believe in God or some supreme being, but they do not indicate that we believe in lots of gods — that has never been a part of our culture. The Greeks had them; the Romans had them; the ancient Egyptians, who had been the masters of Israel for so many years, had them; the Canaanites, whose land Israel would soon inhabit, had them; but we do not. Perhaps the just-freed former slaves of Israel needed this word, but do we? After all, we are modern, scientific — we know that there is no sun god or wind god or rain god. For that matter, some would say that our generation seems to have managed its affairs without regard to any god at all. And if the Decalogue is the social justice document that we claim, where is the danger of injustice here? Does this first commandment apply to us?

14

At first glance, no. The majority of America — Christians, Jews, Muslims — says there is *one* God, the all-powerful, all-knowing, ever-present God. Christian belief goes even beyond that: God is expressed as a trinity — as Father, Son, and Holy Spirit — one God but knowable in three distinct ways. That is the God who tells us that we are to have no other. There *is* only one.

But what about a second glance? The commandment seems to acknowledge that there are indeed other gods, and in our more honest moments, we confess that is true. A god is anyone or anything that is our "ultimate concern" in Paul Tillich's phrase. We might not give that god a name like Moloch or Baal or Jupiter or Zeus, but if it supplants the God of heaven as the Lord of the moment, we begin the slide down a slippery slope. It has been suggested that we *say* we are monotheists but we live like we are polytheists.

Who is your god? The ultimate concern for some is the great god, Mammon. Ancient mythology did not actually have one of those, but we can identify him: Money ... possessions ... things. There are probably more Americans today that serve the god of money, possessions, and things more than any other ... including the God of heaven. Church folk are not immune. The accumulation of wealth is a national obsession, not for purposes of hoarding, but for what it can buy. Our standing in society is in many ways dependent upon the things we own. If you happen to own a big yacht or a Rolls Royce or a large estate, our society *thinks* you have "arrived." You might be emotionally, morally, and spiritually bankrupt, but unless you go around attacking little children, America thinks you are great.

Of course, you are not great if Mammon becomes preeminent. The Bible says, "the love of money is a root of all kinds of evil" (1 Timothy 6:10). Lying, cheating, stealing, killing, and the list could go on and on (and we do love our lists) — all to acquire money, possessions, things. But the worst evil of all is when they become the objects of our real worship.

One of the saddest stories in the New Testament is that one which recounts the meeting between Jesus and the rich young ruler (Matthew 19:16-22; Mark 10:17-22; Luke 18:18-27). The young man came to Jesus asking how he might inherit eternal life. Jesus mentioned the commandments: no murder, no adultery, no stealing, no false testimony, honor to parents; and the man said, "No problem. I have kept all these; what do I still lack?" But then Jesus told him to go and sell what he had and give the proceeds to the poor. At that, the man's face fell, for the scripture says, "he had many possessions." His possessions had come to possess him. They had become his god. But the God of heaven says, "You shall have no other gods before me."

One of the gods that ancient Rome worshiped was named Mercury. He was the messenger god and had oversight of business and commerce. There are still many who worship him without calling him by name. Business is the ultimate concern. If a conflict comes up between family and business, business wins out. If it is between business and relaxation, business wins. "Business before pleasure," as they say. If it is a choice between business and the church, there *is* no choice. Business comes first.

Years ago, a man who had been successful in business proposed this honest epitaph for his tombstone: "Born, 1878, a human being; Died, 1954, a wholesale grocer." A friend asked him what prompted such a request, and he replied, "I have been so busy selling groceries and amassing riches that I have pushed practically everything else out of my life. I have been successful, but so busy making a living, I never had time to live."

The ancient Greeks were another culture that worshiped many gods. Scholars have counted upward of 30,000 of them. Their homes and cities had monuments to them everywhere, because they wanted none to be offended. They even erected one monument to one they called "the unknown god" to make sure that if they had missed any, he or she would not be angry with them (Acts 17:23). One of the best known of the Greek gods is one that is still worshiped today: Bacchus, the god of pleasure.

Be clear about this, there is nothing wrong with pleasure. There are some who would have us believe that anything remotely smacking of fun is wrong. The Puritans were like that. They went so far as to outlaw any celebration of Christmas. Even today there are those who think of God as some sort of grey-bearded, scowling

16

celestial Scrooge sitting up in the sky somewhere looking around hoping to catch someone having fun so he can *zap* them. Nothing could be further from the truth. There is nothing in scripture that says there is anything inherently sinful about enjoying ourselves. Pleasure is only sinful when it is sin, when we break God's laws in its pursuit. But some have made the pursuit of pleasure their god.

The list of gods we worship could go on and on. After all, as we say, we do love our lists. But there is no need for the list to be unending for it to be a problem. All it needs is to have one more name on it than the God of heaven.

Think of those other gods and we begin to understand the justice issues involved. Look at the mess the great god Mammon has caused for those who have chased after him. There is so much dissatisfaction in life because of the mad dash to acquire more and more, just to keep up with the Joneses and then never quite making it. Or look at what Mercury has done — family, friends, church, loving relationships all lost because too much time and had to be expended to keep up with the competition. Or Bacchus — thousands dead and injured on America's highways every year because of drunk drivers; how many young people hooked on drugs; a worldwide AIDS epidemic that threatens to become the worst health disaster that humanity has ever known. "You shall have no other gods before me," because those gods can ruin you.

"You shall have no other gods before me." The command of a maladjusted, anxiety-ridden deity? Hardly. This is the word of a God who loves us with a love that is beyond our understanding — a God who, like a devoted parent, loves us enough to warn us away from the things that endanger us. It is not so much that you will go to hell for having other gods, you will simply feel like you are already there.

"You shall have no other gods before me." When you think about it, who would ever want any?

Study Questions

1. If the vast majority of Americans believe in God, as the polls routinely indicate, why is church attendance as low as it is? What could be done to improve it?

2. Is religion losing influence in our culture? Why or why not?

3. What are some of the other "gods" out there in addition to the ones noted in the text?

4. What are the consequences of ignoring God?

5. With this as the first commandment, can those who wish to display the Decalogue in public buildings legitimately say they are not religious in nature?

------

1. William J. Carl III, "The Decalogue in Liturgy, Preaching, and Life," *Interpretation: A Journal of Bible and Theology*, Vol. XLIII, No. 3 (Richmond, Virginia: Union Theological Seminary in Virginia, 1989), p. 272.

2. See Exodus 22:20; 23:24; and 34:14 for the penal equivalents.

Second Commandment

No Idols!

All who make idols are nothing, and the things they treasure are worthless. Those who would speak up for them are blind; they are ignorant, to their own shame. Who shapes a god and casts an idol, which can profit him nothing? He and his kind will be put to shame; craftsmen are nothing but men. Let them all come together and take their stand; they will be brought down to terror and infamy. The blacksmith takes a tool and works with it in the coals; he shapes an idol with hammers, he forges it with the might of his arm. He gets hungry and loses his strength; he drinks no water and grows faint. The carpenter measures with a line and makes an outline with a marker; he roughs it out with chisels and marks it with compasses. He shapes it in the form of man, of man in all his glory, that it may dwell in a shrine. He cut down cedars, or perhaps took a cypress or oak. He let it grow among the trees of the forest, or planted a pine, and the rain made it grow. It is man's fuel for burning; some of it he takes and warms himself, he kindles a fire and bakes bread. But he also fashions a god and worships it; he makes an idol and bows down to it. Half of the wood he burns in the fire; over it he prepares his meal, he roasts his meat and eats his fill. He also warms himself and says, "Ah! I am warm; I see the fire." From the rest he makes a god, his idol; he bows down to it and worships. He prays to it and says, "Save me; you are my god."
— Isaiah 44:9-17

Can you imagine yourself doing something like that? Turning half a log into firewood and the other half into a god, an object for worship? Pretty dumb, or what? We are much too sophisticated to do any such thing, and to be honest, we are tempted to wonder if those folks way back when who took pieces of wood or stone and ended up bowing down to them might not have had an ancient screw loose. Go figure. How could they have done that?

Well, we ought not to be so smug. Those first idol-makers were very innocent in what they did and very devout at the same time. They were deep thinkers who realized that there were powers or even *a* power in the universe much larger than they. They could see lightning, hear thunder, feel the wind and realized early on that something very special was going on, something that deserved hearty respect — even reverence.

They wanted to express what they felt. But how could that reverence be put into words? There *were* no words. At best, there were mental pictures — the lightning flashed like the tongue of a serpent, the thunder roared like a gigantic lion, the wind blew with the swiftness of the hawk. So these devout folks put knife to wood or chisel to stone and gave those mental pictures some substance. Of course, they knew that serpents and lions and hawks were not God. God was bigger than any of those. So the images took on grotesque forms, not to say that God was grotesque, just that God was greater than those things that people saw every day. That was pretty good theology.

When their work was finished, were they worshiping strange looking serpents or lions or hawks? Of course not. All these statuettes and figurines were simply a way of expressing the inexpressible, a way to make visible the presence of an invisible God. Images were a means to an end. When we think of it that way, idol-making does not sound all that foolish anymore, not even in the twenty-first century.

You may be familiar with Woody Allen's critically acclaimed film, *Hannah And Her Sisters*.[1] Near the end of the movie, Woody was asked by one of the sisters why he had been so out of touch recently, and he responded like this:

> *One day about a month ago I really hit bottom. You know, I just felt that, in a godless universe, who wants*

20

to go on living? Now, I happen to own a rifle ... which I loaded, believe it or not, pressed it to my forehead ... and I remember thinking that I'm gonna kill myself. Then I thought, "What if I'm wrong? What if there really is a God?" I mean, after all, nobody really knows that. Then I thought, "No, maybe is not good enough. I want certainty or nothing."

Woody sat there frozen, gun to his head, debating whether or not to shoot. All of a sudden the gun went off — he had been so tense that his finger squeezed the trigger. But he was perspiring so much that the gun barrel had slipped off his forehead and he blew a hole in his wall — good old Woody.

Now, I confess that I do not think of Woody Allen as a significant theologian. But if there is any modern statement that explains why people would make idols — even dumb ones — Woody's is as good as any. In an uncertain world, a world where jobs always hang by a thread, a world where the stock market makes wild roller coasters seem tame, a world of terrorist threats, a world with political moorings coming loose amidst Washington scandals and fruitless searches for weapons of mass destruction, we crave certainty. We need to feel confidence in something or else we go bonkers and start looking for rifles.

To be sure, having a good idol around can fill that bill. Back in the ancient world this was a god with which people could deal, a god they could see and touch. If the crops would begin to dry up for lack of rain, the people could come to the idol and make their prayer. If an enemy were laying siege to the town, they could come to the idol and call for deliverance. Of course, those early theologians knew that the statue could not answer prayers, but it was comforting to have something visible and touchable there, something reassuring in the midst of difficulty, something more than Woody Allen's *maybe*, to represent what they were convinced was the larger reality.

But as with so many things we human beings do that start out in perfect innocence, it did not take long for that kind of reverence to degenerate. And this is where we begin to get to the social justice issue that is at the heart of all Ten Commandments. Think of the idol-maker's little children. When times were rough and the crops needed help or the enemy was about to storm the gates, the youngsters saw Daddy go in and talk to that statue. Hmm! To the immature young mind, there would be no distinction between the idol and the god it was supposed to represent — the image would *become* God.

It is not hard to figure what would happen as those children grew — they would take their early understanding (or *misunderstanding*) with them and expand on it. They would no longer be content to just come and make their prayers in front of their little shrine, they would come prepared to make deals. "Mr. Idol — Mr. Baal — Mr. Moloch, if you will do this for me, I will do this for you. You want me to dance? Okay, I'll dance. You want me to cut myself with a knife? Okay, Martha, bring me a knife. You want me to slash the throat of my firstborn son? Well, okay, if that is what it takes to make things right."

What had begun in one generation as a representation of something holy, in the minds of succeeding generations would *become* holy — the means would become the end. The idol would become a sanctified rabbit's foot — as long as you have that idol in the house (or town) and you went through the proper rituals, things would be all right — no maybes, no uncertainty. What had begun in perfect innocence and reverence would have now degenerated to the ritual murder of little babies. To mislead people to such an extent is ultimately unjust.

This was the kind of a world into which a rag-tag band of former Egyptian slaves would come to form a new nation, Israel. And it was the religion of this kind of world from which Israel's God, the God of all the universe, wanted to protect the chosen people. Enter the Ten Commandments, and number two in particular:

> *You shall not make for yourself an idol in the form of anything in heaven above or on the earth beneath or in the waters below. You shall not bow down to them or worship them; for I, the Lord your God, am a jealous God, punishing the children for the sin of the fathers to*

the third and fourth generation of those who hate me,
but showing love to a thousand generations of those
who love me and keep my commandments.[2]

That seems pretty clear — no more carved statues. And frankly, if the Hebrew word is to be taken seriously, we would have to say no other statues either, no portraits or photographs, no images of any kind. In other words, no graphic arts. That is what it sounds like.

That was the issue during the Reformation over whether or not statues were permitted in church.[3] The Roman Catholic argument was that statues of the saints were valuable in instructing the people who are reminded by them of what they believe and are inspired by the stories behind them. They are like books for those who cannot read. The Reformers disagreed and insisted that having statues in church would lead to their veneration even though people might be specifically instructed that such should not be. The truly loving thing would be to get rid of the statues so folks would not be tempted. They suggested it would be like a parent standing idly by while a young child plays with a sharp knife. Too dangerous to take the chance. Well, as you can tell by going into Protestant and Catholic churches today, neither side convinced the other.

"You shall not make for yourself an idol," or in the language of the King James Version in which many of us were nurtured, "Thou shalt not make unto thee any graven image." What does it mean? Before that, we should consider what it does NOT mean. It does not mean that we should not have any paintings or sculpture or photographs (although some traditions have interpreted it that way). There were artists in the days when this commandment was given, and there were never any instructions that they should find other work. When it came time for the construction of the tabernacle, God said only the *best* artists and craftsmen should be used for the job. Over the Ark of Covenant God told them to sculpt two magnificent images of angels (Exodus 25:18-20). On the hem of the robe of the high priest, God instructed that tailors include likenesses of pomegranates and bells (Exodus 28:33-34). If no images of any kind were allowed, God would never have had these things

23

done — God is not self-contradictory. So the implication is clear: God does not object to images, but when they are made as objects of worship, God calls a halt.

One would think that such a commandment would not be very hard to keep. I remember the story of a young man coming out of worship one day when the sermon had dealt with the Ten Commandments. A friend asked how it had gone and he replied shaking his head, "Well, at least I haven't made any graven images." The whole idea of making something with your own hands for the sole purpose of worshiping it sounds ridiculous. The prophet Isaiah laughed at it; the letter of Jeremiah in the Apocrypha is hilarious in its sarcasm. But on the other hand, there is nothing more natural than taking something that we think of as a representation of the divine or divine power and allowing ourselves to give it a reverential importance far beyond what it actually has. That is why, in the whole Bible, there are more references to this second commandment than to any of the others.

The story of the brass serpent in the wilderness is a perfect example. In Numbers 21, we read the account of an attack on a grumbling nation of Israel by poisonous snakes. The people were dying like flies until Moses asked God for help. So God instructed Moses to have a brass serpent fashioned so that those who looked on it might live. So far, so good. The next time we hear anything about that brass serpent is in 2 Kings 18. Over the centuries that separate the two accounts, the people had come to start looking on that snake as something more than simply a reminder of God's power; they had begun to worship it and were even burning incense to it. It got so bad that King Hezekiah smashed the thing into little pieces. It had become an idol, just like the grotesque hawks and lions and serpents of centuries before. What had started out as a *reminder* of God finally had *become* a god. The means had become the end.

People still do it. They look at something that represents security and fulfillment, the kinds of things that a gracious God would be thought of as providing, and they begin to credit them with inordinate value. Not gods carved from wood or stone, but big houses, flashy cars, a million shares of Microsoft, the trappings of success.

The means and ends have become confused once again. People make sacrifices of time, talent, treasure, and even the welfare of their children to those material gods in ways which would have made the ancient idol-makers think us just as absurd as we think them. Idolatry is still around; it has become a bit fancier, that's all. And the ultimate injustice of it is as strong as ever.

In the venerable *McGuffey's Reader* is the old fable about the miser who had a sub-basement under his regular basement, known only to himself, where he kept his silver and gold. Each day he would come down and run his bony fingers through the coins and say, "My beauties, oh, my beauties." One day the wind howled through that basement and blew the door of the sub-basement shut with the man inside. The door was fastened with a spring lock which could only be turned from the outside — no way out. Years later when the house was torn down, the workmen found a skeleton draped over a heap of coins. Money had become his security, his idol, and his idol had destroyed him.

"You shall not make for yourself an idol." There is one other reason for that prohibition, and it is simply this: *No* representation, no image of the Lord of the whole universe could possibly convey the whole story. Any representation would be, at best, incomplete. And sometimes, in its incompleteness, the image could be a blatant misrepresentation.

Good church folk do it all the time. This beautiful cross that graces our sanctuary ... or for that matter, the shiny crosses that we wear on necklaces or lapels — are they idols? To be sure, the cross of Jesus Christ is central to our faith, but what about a polished, clean, lovely cross? The cross was a horrible thing, the first century equivalent of an electric chair or a syringe with a lethal injection. Who would think of gold-plating one of those? But we have done it with the cross.

Or even with the Bible. We say it is the word of God. As the bumper stickers have it, "The Bible Says It; I Believe It; That Settles it." Simple — *too* simple — because it is too easy to defend almost any position one wishes to take by quoting the words of scripture. "Cain killed his brother Abel" (Genesis 4:8). "Go and do likewise" (Deuteronomy 22:3). "What thou doest, do quickly"

25

(John 13:27 KJV). The Bible says...! The Bible says...! We call that sin "Bibliolatry."

"You shall not make for yourself an idol." You see how easy it is? God warns what will happen if we do. The sin will be passed on to our kids and theirs after them, in just the way the children of the ancients got confused while watching Daddy pray at the idol's feet. The text says, "... punishing the children for the sin of the fathers to the third and fourth generation...." That does not mean our great-grandchildren will, all of a sudden, be penalized for something we did years ago. That would be unjust in itself. But it does mean that, so many times, the consequences of our sins are passed on, the same way that a mother with AIDS or a father in jail pass on misery to their children. The justice issue arises again.

Fortunately, there is one more part to this second commandment — a promise: "... but showing love to a thousand generations of those who love me and keep my commandments," which parallels and contrasts the third and fourth generation reference in the warning. What a marvelous contrast it is, too. God's love is infinitely greater than God's anger. If we keep God's commandments, not only our children and grandchildren will know that love, but untold generations in the future will, also. It was that kind of love that sent Jesus to the cross. And it is that same kind of love that brings us to salvation ... wholeness ... life.

Near the end of Woody Allen's movie, after his complaint about life's uncertainty and his abortive suicide, he says, "Maybe is a very slim reed to hang your whole life on, but it is the best we have." Is it? I hope not. We are not likely to take a log and use half for firewood and the other half to make a god in our quest for certainty as the ancients did. No, the certainty for us, and for Christians throughout the ages, is in faith ... faith in a loving Lord, one who loved us so much that he died that we might live.

No idols. No matter. Don't need any anyway.

Study Questions

1. Are there other idols to which people cling besides those mentioned in the text?

2. The text mentions the Bible as a possible idol — how about the church building? How about specific doctrinal interpretations? What other things about our religious practices can tempt us to elevate them to "idol" status?

3. How do we answer those who say any literal representation of something such as photographs or sculptures, violates this commandment?

4. What are the signs of idolatry — signs that we are worshiping something other than God?

5. We often use symbols to aid our worship (bread, wine, water, candles, and the like). Can they become an "idolatry" problem?

6. How are we to understand God's jealousy?

---

1. *Hannah And Her Sisters*, Orion Pictures, 1986, Robert Greenhut, producer; written and directed by Woody Allen.

2. See Exodus 34:17; Leviticus 19:4; and Deuteronomy 4:9-12, 16, 23, 25; 27:15 for the penal code equivalent.

3. David C. Steinmetz, "The Reformation and the Ten Commandments," *Interpretation: A Journal of Bible and Theology*, Vol. XLIII, No. 3 (Richmond, Virginia: Union Theological Seminary in Virginia, 1989), pp. 256-266.

Third Commandment

God's Name

Again, you have heard that it was said to the people long ago, "Do not break your oath, but keep the oaths you have made to the Lord." But I tell you, Do not swear at all: either by heaven, for it is God's throne; or by the earth, for it is his footstool; or by Jerusalem, for it is the city of the Great King. And do not swear by your head, for you cannot make even one hair white or black. Simply let your "Yes" be "Yes," and your "No," "No"; anything beyond this comes from the evil one.
— Matthew 5:33-37

In the NIV, Exodus 20:7 says, "You shall not misuse the name of the Lord your God, for the Lord will not hold anyone guiltless who misuses his name."[1] Or, as the venerable King James has it, "Thou shalt not take the name of the Lord thy God in vain...."

As you are probably aware, for the past number of years, there have been some billboards along the nation's highways that sometimes refer to the Ten Commandments. There is the one that asks, "What Part of 'Thou Shalt Not ...' don't you understand?" Signed, "God." Drivers on a jammed commuter road face this warning: "Keep using my name in vain, I'll make rush hour longer," also signed simply "God." I am not sure if anyone has ever come forward to admit to paying for the campaign, but they surely have gotten people's attention.

"You shall not misuse of the name of the Lord your God." Is that the "misuse" of God's name this commandment is talking about? The rhetoric of road rage? Or just the casual cursing that we hear whenever someone is coarse enough to use it?

Granted, that *is* what most of us (and the billboard advertiser, obviously) have been taught. We insult a holy and righteous God when we use the divine name loosely. Not only might we go to hell, Momma might wash our mouth out with soap in preparation for our descent into the abyss. That teaching is not exactly correct.

The problem is language. We grew up hearing the prohibition against using the Lord's name *in vain*. But, in modern speech, the phrase *in vain* implies failure. If Barry Bonds or Albert Pujols did not hit home runs in the games last night, the sportscasts this morning could say their attempts were *in vain*. No homers. Or if a young man sends flowers and candy and all sorts of indications of affection to the girl of his dreams, but she does not respond appropriately, we say his gifts were *in vain*. A failure. But using the name of the Lord *in vain*? Failure? That makes no sense.

What else could it mean? We can go back to the Elizabethan English of the King James Version. We recall "Vanity of vanities, saith the preacher ..." from Ecclesiastes. Vanity there means "nothingness" or "emptiness" or "meaningless." Perhaps a clue there. "You shall not use the name of the Lord your God in a meaningless way" — casual cursing, and so on. Now we find the source of those lessons from our childhood.

The problem is those lessons missed the heart of the commandment. The Hebrew words behind vanity in Ecclesiastes and in vain here in Exodus are different. The Ecclesiastes word (*hebel*) does indeed imply emptiness or meaninglessness; the Exodus word (from *shav'*) has an evil connotation to it and refers to guile and deception. Rather than a word indicating flippancy, this one indicates an active attempt to do harm. Now we begin to understand a bit more. The more modern translations of the commandment, "You shall not make wrongful use of the name of the Lord your God ..." as the NRSV has it, or "You shall not misuse the name ..." in the NIV are quite correct. They retain Grandmother's prohibition against using God's name as a casual curse while expanding into the realm of insuring that God's name is not used as active support for evil or injustice. And here is where the rubber really meets the road. If the Ten Commandments is, at heart, a social justice document, we begin to see the real thrust of this word.

One final thought here on this use of God's name as an expletive: the fact that this is *not* what prompted the commandment is all the more obvious when we know that the last thing an Israelite man or woman would have considered saying was something as frivolous as "God dammit." This was the name of the one they worshiped. Throw that name around casually in conversation? Not on your life. If an Israelite had said "God damn anything," he would have meant it. It would not have been a statement; it would have been a prayer.

Back to what the commandment really does mean. One of the better renderings of the ancient instruction is this: "Thou shalt not lift up the name of YAHWEH for mischief."[2]

What kind of mischief? Several kinds actually. And all are tied up with just how seriously the ancients took any invocation of God's name. For example, the situation that prompted Jesus' own commentary on this commandment in the Sermon on the Mount — taking an oath. Lines such as, "As God is my witness, I promise to ... do this or that," or "May God strike me dead, if I fail to ... do this or that." The idea is that God is offered as guarantor of the promise.

Ah, but human beings are clever, especially when falling to our baser instincts. "O what a tangled web we weave when first we practice to deceive."[3] As background to this, remember how seriously the ancient world took the mention of the name of God. Indeed, some of the faithful Jews of Jesus' day, to avoid any possibility of breaking the commandment, refused to use the names of Yahweh or Elohim at all. They would go so far as to call God simply "the Name." If they took an oath, they would swear in "the name of the Name." They would be especially scrupulous about promising anything in the name of God that they had no intention of doing.

Now, the clever part. For the Jews, the only oaths thought to be irrevocable were the ones taken in the name of God. After all, there was this third commandment to consider. Any others were worth as much as the individual cared to make them. Knowing this, there was a little subterfuge that occasionally went on. Some would swear by "heaven" to give the impression that the oath was binding, when indeed, they would not consider it so because the actual name of God had not been used. Or they would swear by everything on earth or their own head, by anything to keep from using God's name ... all because they wanted to be free to keep or break the promise as they saw fit. Jesus said not to swear that you are going to do something or not do something; if you say you will, do it; if you say you won't, don't. And, at its heart, that was the reason for this third commandment in the first place, because basic honesty is one of the building blocks of a just society. Simple justice demands that we be able to trust each other to keep our word.

We would do well to remember that. We take marriage vows and then keep or break them at our whim. We take vows at the baptism of our children to raise them "in the knowledge and love of God," and then fail to keep the pledge. We go to work for an employer, giving an implied pledge in accepting the job, that we will provide an honest day's work for an honest day's pay ... unless we can get away with less. Jesus' message is, if you make a pledge, keep it ... whether you swear by the name of God or not.

Another issue. There was a certain practice in the religions of the East that surrounded the nation of Israel that involved the over-and-over repetition of the name of their god in an almost magical incantation. The one doing the chanting would, in some mysterious way, be drawing some of that god's power down to himself or herself. It was all a part of that ancient belief that if you knew someone's name, whatever power that one might have over you might somehow be diminished and turned over to you. The name of the god was used like we might use "Abracadabra," for magic, and God says not to do that.

Whether we realize it or not, that kind of usage occurs even in the church. Do you ever run across folks who punctuate almost every sentence with "Praise the Lord" or "Praise God"? Now, there is obviously nothing wrong with praising the Lord. But when a phrase is used over and over and over again, there is danger that the phrase is being used, not to praise the Lord, but to let anyone within earshot know how pious I am and as a password to insure my acceptance among the devout. If that is what someone thinks they need to establish their *bona fides*, I would be concerned. Be careful around them.

"You shall not use the name of the Lord your God for mischief." One more issue in this third commandment, and it is as up to date as tomorrow's newspaper. Perjury. "Do you swear to tell the truth, the whole truth and nothing but the truth, so help you God?"

"I do."

We have all seen movies and television programs where those courtroom scenes were depicted. If a witness came up with some questionable testimony, the lawyer might remind them, "Remember, you are under oath," inferring that all of heaven was watching to make sure the truth was told. A fair and effective judicial system in any society is dependent on the truthfulness of participants, and we get an affirmation of that specifically in the eighth commandment against bearing false witness. This third commandment insists on it as well.

"You shall not make wrongful use of the name of the Lord your God," not in insincere pledges, not for magic, not in court, and certainly not as a casual curse. A corollary could well be, "You *shall* take the name of your God" — in other words, God's power, God's majesty, God's character, everything that you think of when you hear God's name — "you *shall* take God's name SERIOUSLY." When we do, it makes all the difference.

The message here is that this God cares deeply about the things that fashion our life. A Bible study group was about to delve into the swamps of Leviticus, and one of the participants, a young gay man, began the discussion by saying, "Because of my sexual orientation, I have always feared reading this book of the Bible. We all know that Leviticus is against gays. Right? Well, to my surprise, Leviticus is against a lot of things! I found rules in here for how to cook, how to eat, how to treat farm animals. The amazing thing to me is how concerned God is about so many little, everyday domestic problems! What kind of God would care about how we have sex, even more about how we make dinner?"[4] What kind of God? A God with standards.

That being said, we who worship this God then will not be content with the standards of the world. We will share a gospel that is genuinely *good news*, not bad — not just a billboard-type religion that asks "What part of 'Thou shalt not' do you not understand?" Instead, the emphasis will be on the very good news that Jesus loves us, has paid our penalty for sin, and invites us to life with him in the kingdom of God. We will work for justice, oppose discrimination, fight oppression, and try to put meat on the bones of that ancient and honored concept called "love thy neighbor." We will look forward to the day when, "at the name of Jesus every knee should bow, in heaven and on earth and under the earth, and every tongue confess that Jesus Christ is Lord, to the glory of God the Father" (Philippians 2:10-11).

Are you ready for that? What a day it will be! In the poetry of scripture, "Every valley shall be filled, and every mountain and hill shall be made low, and the crooked shall be made straight, and the rough ways made smooth; and all flesh shall see the salvation of God" (Luke 3:5-6 NRSV). What a day! Are you ready? Come, Lord Jesus.

Study Questions

1. Besides those mentioned by the author, what are ways we misuse/make wrongful use of God's name?

2. Who is hurt when we misuse God's name?

3. If we imply that God is with us, then who is God against?

4. If this commandment is ultimately not against using God's name as an expletive, how do we get people to "clean up" their speech?

5. Is there a place for vows in the name of God in our culture? Why or why not?

1. See Leviticus 6:3, 5; 19:12 for the penal code equivalent of this commandment.

2. Walter Harrelson, *The Ten Commandments and Human Rights* (Philadelphia: Fortress Press, 1980), p. 72.

3. Sir Walter Scott, "Introduction to Marmion," Canto VI, Stanza 17, *Marmion: A Tale of Flodden Field* (New York: Cosimo Classics, 2005), p. 244.

4. Stanley Hauerwas and William Willimon, *The Truth About God: The Ten Commandments in Christian Life* (Nashville: Abingdon, 1990), pp. 43-44.

The Sabbath

One Sabbath Jesus was going through the grainfields, and as his disciples walked along, they began to pick some heads of grain. The Pharisees said to him, "Look, why are they doing what is unlawful on the Sabbath?"

He answered, "Have you never read what David did when he and his companions were hungry and in need? In the days of Abiathar the high priest, he entered the house of God and ate the consecrated bread, which is lawful only for priests to eat. And he also gave some to his companions."

Then he said to them, "The Sabbath was made for man, not man for the Sabbath. So the Son of Man is Lord even of the Sabbath."

Another time he went into the synagogue, and a man with a shriveled hand was there. Some of them were looking for a reason to accuse Jesus, so they watched him closely to see if he would heal him on the Sabbath. Jesus said to the man with the shriveled hand, "Stand up in front of everyone."

Then Jesus asked them, "Which is lawful on the Sabbath: to do good or to do evil, to save life or to kill?" But they remained silent. He looked around at them in anger and, deeply distressed at their stubborn hearts, said to the man, "Stretch out your hand."

He stretched it out, and his hand was completely restored. Then the Pharisees went out and began to plot with the Herodians how they might kill Jesus.

— Mark 2:23—3:6

Let me tell you a story.[1] It seems a young Martian was studying comparative anthropology and, in preparation for a doctoral dissertation which was long overdue, made a quick flight down to

Earth in his flying saucer to check on the habits of the residents of the planet. He could not get too close or make any prolonged inspection because his work had to be submitted in just a few days, so time was of the essence. He had made a fortunate choice of days and locations — a fine summer Sunday over the United States — and found the natives most obligingly coming out of their houses and spreading themselves all over the landscape for his observation.

The first thing he noted was that, like so many primitive life forms, the people of this planet were sun worshipers. Previous research had indicated that one day in seven was set aside for the adoration of their god (weather permitting). The rituals would vary, and each required a different form of dress, but most all were conducted in the open air.

What the student saw fascinated him. Some creatures gathered in vast arenas to watch strangely garbed priests perform elaborate ceremonies involving a ball (which every Martian school child knows is symbolic of the sun), some strangely shaped pieces of wood and certain ritual expressions chanted either by certain priests (like "Stee-rike one!") and occasional responses from the worshipers (like "Kill the umpire," whatever that means). There were even appointed times during the service for the worshipers to rhythmically stand and then quickly sit creating a great human wave as if to pay homage to some unseen god of the sea (perhaps a brother or sister to the sun god).

Speaking of the sea, others stripped themselves almost naked, went down to the shore, and performed their rites there. Often they would hurl themselves into the waves with frenzied cries. Many would carry with them, as might be expected, a ball, this one brightly colored. Then after the ceremonial immersion, the devotees would anoint themselves with holy oil, stretch out full length with eyes closed, and present themselves as a soon-to-be-burnt offering to the deity.

Still other earth creatures, no doubt the mystics and solitaries of their religion, either by themselves or in groups of two or four, dressed in gaily colored liturgical garments, traveled to quiet fields for their ritual. There they would place their ball on the ground, hit it with a long stick, chase after it, and hit it again until it finally would fall into the hole of some underground animal. It struck the Martian student as a rather strange process because after striking the ball the worshiper would often chant "Go in, Go in," but once it went in, they would promptly take the ball *out* and repeat the effort all over again.

Another group apparently had blood sacrifice as a part of their tradition. Thousands gathered in huge sanctuaries, semi-clothed, most sipping a foamy sacramental beverage from shiny cylindrical containers (which appeared to the Martian, by the way, to cross all religious lines — all righteous earthlings seemed to share this practice). This throng would watch their priests enter large and noisy wheeled cubicles called cars which they propelled round in circles at terrific speed until one of the priests would be injured or killed. The worshipers frequently mimicked the practice outside the sanctuary with their own cars, running them at high speeds until they dashed themselves to bits against other cars or stationary objects. Many, particularly after one of their religious services, would enter their cars in unison and thus be too closely packed to move. They would then allow the sun god's rays to beat down on the metal which then cooked them slowly to death.

Finally, there was a small group of dissenters or heretics which did not practice sun worship. These could be identified by their habit of clothing themselves much more soberly and completely than the sun worshipers. They, too, gathered in groups (albeit much smaller groups) but they congregated in buildings, many of which had colored windows which blocked the light making certain that there would be no temptation toward sun worship. It was not clear to the student whether these buildings were places of punishment or not, nor was it clear whether these creatures had been excommunicated from the larger worship community or were simply unbelievers. The one thing that was clear was that their faces and gestures showed none of the joyful religious ecstasy with which the sun worshipers pursued their devotions. The only conclusion which the Martian felt could be legitimately drawn was that this poor group was obviously not happy. And so ended one extraterrestrial student's adventure.

One is forced to wonder: was the Martian wildly wrong or wildly right? We would have to admit that his descriptions of Sunday activities are easily recognized.

To be sure, Americans do think of Sunday as a special day, a holiday, a "holy" day, a day set apart from the rest of the week. But no longer is it "holy" or set apart as it was when many of us were growing up. We heard our preachers solemnly intone the fourth commandment:

> *Remember the Sabbath day by keeping it holy. Six days you shall labor and do all your work, but the seventh day is a Sabbath to the Lord your God. On it you shall not do any work, neither you, nor your son or daughter, nor your manservant or maidservant, nor your animals, nor the alien within your gates. For in six days the Lord made the heavens and the earth, the sea, and all that is in them, but he rested on the seventh day. Therefore the Lord blessed the Sabbath day and made it holy.*[2]

I do not know whether you noticed it, but in that list of all those who are not supposed to work on the sabbath, there is no mention of mother. For the one who has had to get the breakfast, the children, the dinner, and herself ready to try to make it to church almost on time, this is hardly a day of no work. But then, the scripture never said it would be ... not for Mom. The Bible never expects the impossible.

At any rate, those sermons we always heard about keeping the sabbath were not really about the sabbath — the seventh day, Saturday — they were talking about Sunday. But was that right? Nowhere in the Bible is there any instruction for Christians to consider the Lord's Day as a replacement for the Jewish Sabbath. The Reformers were clear on that: Luther liked the principle of a day off each week for rest, refreshment, and worship but said it did not matter which day; Calvin said, "The Jewish holy day was abolished ... the observance of days among us is a free service and void of all superstition."[3] Still, we were taught that Sunday had become the new sabbath anyway. And it resulted in a set of restrictions being set around Sundays that were almost as bad as the over-1,500 which the Jews had placed around the sabbath.

You have heard about some of those Jewish regulations, no doubt. For example, under the general law, "You shall bear no burden on the sabbath," the scribes solemnly set down, as a by-law, that while a woman could have a ribbon sewn onto her dress, it must not be merely pinned on. If it were only pinned, it was not secure enough to be considered a part of the dress, and in wearing the ribbon with a pin, she was carrying a burden. Under the same heading, it was decreed that false teeth were not to be worn on the sabbath ... they were a burden.

In Mark's gospel, the Pharisees complained to Jesus that his disciples were gathering corn on the sabbath ... reaping. That was work, a violation of the fourth commandment. But consider this: a woman was not allowed to use a mirror on the sabbath to prevent exactly the same sin: reaping. You see, they were concerned that she would see a gray hair and pull it out, and pulling out gray hairs was reaping. The healing of the man with the withered hand? Jesus put that in perspective with his question, "Which is lawful on the sabbath: to do good or to do evil, to save life or to kill?" Yes, healing is work — ask any nurse or doctor. But....

No wonder Jesus got into trouble. He hated sham and hypocrisy; he despised displays of righteousness. When it came to the observance of the sabbath, he put everything into perspective in one sentence: "The sabbath was made for man, not man for the sabbath." All those ridiculous restrictions had nothing to do with God's intention in giving the commandment. This was social justice policy to guarantee that people would not be overworked. There is nothing in it that talks about wearing ribbons or false teeth or pulling gray hairs or even healing; there is nothing in it about going to church or synagogue; there is nothing in it about avoiding certain kinds of physical recreation; all it really says is that there should be a day set apart — kept "holy" — different — for folks to take a break.

Jesus would probably have gotten into just as much trouble with church folks through the years. After all, beginning in about

41

the eighth century, our people began that identification of the sabbath with Sunday and ended up doing to Sunday almost as much as the orthodox Jews did, and still do, to Saturday.

For a while, having Sunday thought of as different was easy. In America, for example, the traditional 11 a.m. worship hour that many churches still observe was set to accommodate farmers who, considering morning chores and travel time by horse and wagon, could not arrive until that hour. A two-hour service might be followed by a picnic lunch on the church grounds. Then a period of Bible study (Sunday school, if you will), another time of music and worship, a picnic supper, a vesper service, and finally the long trip home. (For those who call for a return to the "Old Time Religion," this is what they would have if they got their way.) Sunday was automatically special because there was no time for anything *but* church. Society was geared to that, so no one planned to conduct business on that day. Everyone was otherwise occupied.

But as the rural character of the nation changed, as transportation became more efficient, people had more time to do things on Sunday besides go to church. Businesses began to operate since there were opportunities to "make a buck" that had not existed before. Sports events began to be scheduled on Sunday afternoons because folks were no longer spending that time in church.

Of course, there were raised eyebrows among the faithful. There were attempts to legislate reverence for the Lord's Day with the enactment of Blue Laws which tried (unsuccessfully) to force Christianity on everyone. That turned people away from the church rather than toward it. The English writer, John Ruskin, said that Monday morning was the happiest time of the week for him because that meant there were six days until the dreaded, miserable Sunday would come around again. I know the feeling — I grew up not being allowed to do much of anything except church on Sunday (no ball games, no picnics, nothing fun), and it was *boring*!

Of course, some will object, "How will you get people to come to church if they do not have to?" Good question. How are we doing it now? Poorly, obviously. That is why the Martian would see so many sun worshipers. The answer is not in a legalistic approach. Folks will come to church when they feel that doing so really does give them a break, a break from a rat race where it seems that only the rats ever win, a break from a world that does not care whether I live or die, a break from a world full of pain and suffering and hate. Men and women, boys and girls will come when they begin to sense their need of a loving and gracious God and for the company of God's people, a God and a people who care when no one else does. When the churches begin to do a better job of communicating that instead of making folks feel *more* unwanted and unloved than they already feel, people will come. You could not keep them away with clubs.

By the way, as we have noted before, the Ten Commandments are listed virtually identically in both Exodus 20 and Deuteronomy 5. This particular commandment is *not* identical. The Exodus version gives as the rationale for sabbath observance the fact that God rested on the seventh day of creation. But Deuteronomy?

> *Observe the Sabbath day by keeping it holy, as the Lord your God has commanded you. Six days you shall labor and do all your work, but the seventh day is a Sabbath to the Lord your God. On it you shall not do any work, neither you, nor your son or daughter, nor your manservant or maidservant, nor your ox, your donkey or any of your animals, nor the alien within your gates, so that your manservant and maidservant may rest, as you do.* [And here is the kicker.] *Remember that you were slaves in Egypt and that the Lord your God brought you out of there with a mighty hand and an outstretched arm. Therefore the Lord your God has commanded you to observe the Sabbath day.*
> — Deuteronomy 5:12-15

Remember where you came from. You were at the bottom of the heap, but God delivered you. Now that you are on top, do not forget those on the bottom so they do not have to go through what you did.

One of the issues that has been confronting our nation in recent years is illegal immigration, and the problem has become a political football. Despite what some politicians say about how

43

dangerous these folks are and that they can be here only for nefarious purposes, we know that most of them have only come for the
opportunity for the chance at a better life for themselves and their
families and are doing jobs that would go begging if they were left
to Americans. Huge amounts of money flow from these workers
back to countries south of our border to support families who would
be otherwise destitute. Of special interest in that regard is the instruction that Israel heard in this commandment to make sure to
include the immigrant aliens in their sabbath celebration. One wonders what might happen if the church in America would take that
instruction as seriously.

"Remember the sabbath day by keeping it holy — no work —
take a break." This commandment was one of the most gracious
gifts that a loving God could have ever provided. It was as if Yahweh
had created an oasis for Israel in the midst of a weeklong desert.
Then a fence was put around it and a sign on the gate that said,
"Use this oasis freely, but leave the desert outside."

For Christians, by tradition Sunday is our little oasis ... our
place apart in the noisy din of a hectic week. What makes the day
"holy" for you? Worship? Prayer? Praise? Study? Wonderful. Family? Terrific. Recreation? Fine! The point is that it is *up to you*.
Jesus taught that one day in seven was made for you and not you
for the day ... a day to take a break. "Remember the sabbath day
and keep it holy ... set apart; six days you shall labor and do all
your work, but the seventh day" ... ah, the seventh day ... is a gracious, wonderful gift from your lavish, loving Lord.

Study Questions

1. What was sabbath-keeping like when you were younger? How
   has it changed, if at all?

2. If sabbath-keeping is more concerned with "rhythm-of-life"
   issues than religion, how can we get people to come to church?

3. What do you make of the differences in this commandment between Exodus 20 and Deuteronomy 5?

4. What are some of the things we *should* set aside time for, but are routinely ignored?

5. To what do we become enslaved when we fail to keep the sabbath?

---

1. Embellished from a story by Joy Davidman, *Smoke on the Mountain* (Philadelphia: Westminster Press, 1954), pp. 49-51.

2. See Exodus 23:12; 31:12-17; 34:21; 35:2-3; Leviticus 19:3b; 23:3; 26:2; and Numbers 15:32-36 for the penal code equivalent of this commandment.

3. John Calvin, *Institutes of the Christian Religion* (Philadelphia: Westminster Press, 1960), 2.8.32, 34.

Honoring Parents

The Pharisees and some of the teachers of the law who had come from Jerusalem gathered around Jesus and saw some of his disciples eating food with hands that were "unclean," that is, unwashed. (The Pharisees and all the Jews do not eat unless they give their hands a ceremonial washing, holding to the tradition of the elders. When they come from the marketplace they do not eat unless they wash. And they observe many other traditions, such as the washing of cups, pitchers and kettles.) So the Pharisees and teachers of the law asked Jesus, "Why don't your disciples live according to the tradition of the elders instead of eating their food with 'unclean' hands?"

He replied, "Isaiah was right when he prophesied about you hypocrites; as it is written: 'These people honor me with their lips, but their hearts are far from me. They worship me in vain; their teachings are but rules taught by men.' You have let go of the commands of God and are holding on to the traditions of men."

And he said to them: "You have a fine way of setting aside the commands of God in order to observe your own traditions! For Moses said, 'Honor your father and your mother,' and, 'Anyone who curses his father or mother must be put to death.' But you say that if a man says to his father or mother: 'Whatever help you might otherwise have received from me is Corban' (that is, a gift devoted to God), then you no longer let him do anything for his father or mother. Thus you nullify the word of God by your tradition that you have handed down. And you do many things like that."

— Mark 7:1-13

The family. The "basic building block of society" they call it. We are born into families, cared for by family, until we can begin to take care of ourselves. We share the same roof, the same table, even the same faith. Nothing unusual there. It is expected; despite the differences of individual personalities, interests, and abilities that are gathered into the family unit, it is a unit — the basic building block of society.

The joy I have in living with my wife and children I would not have were it not for the institution of the family, and now that we are "empty-nesters," those times when the kids come home are all the more precious. I shared wonderful times with my parents, my sisters, and my brother as we grew up, times that would have been missed except for the family. The family is special, even though we often take it very much for granted.

But being so closely knit, there are problems that are unique to families. As the song goes, "You always hurt the one you love/the one you shouldn't hurt at all." Siblings have their rivalries and sometimes have to be dragged off one another, kicking and screaming. Often, the only time the brothers and sisters are on the same side of anything is when they are united in opposition to their parents.

Grandparents are a problem from the other end. Gramps comes in and sees his little angel, starts fishing around in his pocket, and says, "Let's see if we have some money in here for you." But years before, when you went to him for a nickel, you got the story of how he had to get up at three o'clock in the morning when he was seven years old, walk ten miles in the dark to milk 100 cows. The farmer had no bucket, so he had to squirt the milk into his little hand then travel another eight miles to the nearest milk can, and all for ten cents a week. Forget that nickel. Someone has said the reason grandparents and grandchildren get along so well is that they have common enemies ... Mommy and Daddy.

Despite the fact that those relationships can be great sources of good fun, too often things do work out that other way — as enemies. From time immemorial there have been tensions between generations — one expects deference because "I'm the father and I said so"; the next is convinced that nothing really important happened in the history of the world until *I* came along. Tension. God says be careful. "Honor your father and your mother, so that you may live long in the land the Lord your God is giving you."[1] And be aware, this commandment is directed at *adult* children; this is not aimed at rebellious children who never clean up their rooms.

Why should such a commandment be necessary? To be blunt, in the ancient world, it was dangerous to grow old. In some of the cultures that surrounded the newly freed nation of Israel, aged parents were sent off to die of starvation and exposure in the desert. They had, quite literally, outlived their usefulness. In giving the commandment, God was insisting that the Israelites not pick up this horrible habit of their pagan neighbors. If, at their heart, these Ten Commandments are God's outline for establishing a just society, then this fifth commandment is the "Social Security" legislation. Just societies take care of those who are vulnerable, and that includes aged parents.

So saying, we should note that more than mere tolerance of parents is required here, more than simply allowing them to continue to live. God says, "Honor" your mother and father. The Hebrew term (*kabod*) includes among its definitions "be heavy," suggesting the sense of "give weight to ... gravity ... importance." In other words, treat parents with appropriate seriousness.

How does that play out? If we take someone seriously, we listen to what he or she has to say. We may not automatically agree, but we do listen. For the nation of Israel, one generation listening to the previous generation was crucial — this was the way the culture and the faith were (and still are) passed on. Note the way the instruction is recorded in Deuteronomy. Moses speaks:

> *Now this is the commandment — the statutes and the ordinances — that the Lord your God charged me to teach you to observe in the land that you are about to cross into and occupy, so that you and your children and your children's children may fear the Lord your God all the days of your life, and keep all his decrees and his commandments that I am commanding you, so that your days may be long* [Sound familiar?] *... Keep these words that I am commanding you today in your*

heart. Recite them to your children and talk about them
when you are at home and when you are away, when
you lie down and when you rise....
— Deuteronomy 6:1-7 (NRSV)

"*Honor* your father and your mother...." Take them seriously. Listen to them. They and their generation are the ones who teach you what is ultimately important.

A certain part of "honor" is support. I cannot imagine the ancient world allowing Mom and Dad to just die when no longer commercially useful, but they did. I cannot imagine a child knowingly allowing a parent to do without the necessities of life, but they do. Even in the church.

It was a problem in Jesus' day, too. In Mark's gospel, Jesus condemns the religious leaders who tried to avoid providing for their aging parents by declaring that all their own worldly goods were dedicated to God, *corban*, as it was called. *Corban* in Hebrew means "gift." By declaring property *corban*, it was considered to have already been laid on the altar and therefore, was no longer available for any secular use ... even the care of needy parents. The scribal legalists of the day said this was legitimate. Jesus said this was nuts. Physical support is a part of honor.

No question, problems arise. One more mouth to feed can be a financial burden. Inconvenience? Sometimes aging parents need help in caring for themselves. In *Grimm's Fairy Tales* there is the story of a man who had taken his elderly father into his home. It distressed the son to have to do it and disturbed him that Dad was not as physically capable as he thought the father ought to be. He could not even eat his meals without spilling on the table. The son finally got exasperated and built a trough from which the father was forced to eat to make sure the rest of the table would be spared his lack of coordination. One day the man went into his workshop to find his young son very busy. He asked the boy what he was building. The youngster, with a smile of pride and accomplishment, replied, "Look, Dad, I have made you a trough to eat from when you get old." Honor your father and mother, indeed!

50

From an emotional standpoint, when parents encounter times of stress, the support of children can make a tremendous difference. My mother said many times after my father died, that one of the things that got her through those difficult days, and still helps even today, is the support she feels from her children. Often, aging parents, even though their physical needs are taken care of, feel useless, left out, like a "fifth wheel." Health and physical limitations do not allow them to do everything, so now they feel they are worth nothing. I have no idea how many times I have heard while visiting elderly parishioners, "I wish God would take me; I am only a burden; I just want to die." The children can help — show the parents that they are worth something, that their life has meaning and purpose. That kind of emotional support is a part of honor.

Of course, honor implies respect. In the case of parents, respect involves a certain regard for their position in the family; they were here first, after all. They should be able to expect certain things: to be addressed respectfully, not to be held up to ridicule in the eyes of others, even to be obeyed. Obedience might seem an outmoded concept these days, but the scripture is very clear: "Children, obey your parents in the Lord, for this is right" (Ephesians 6:1). Nowhere is that ever contradicted. A certain wisdom generally comes with age that should not be ignored. When it is, society suffers. Honor and respect for parents make sense.

That good sense resulted in the promise that God made a part of this fifth commandment: "... so that you may live long in the land the Lord your God is giving you." To be truthful, it could have read, "... that your days may not be hastily shortened." In many ancient cultures, parents had the power of life and death over their children. Even in Israel, the penalty for a child cursing his or her parents was death (Leviticus 20:9; Deuteronomy 21:18-21). A father could say to a recalcitrant son, in the Hebrew equivalent of Bill Cosby's words, "Listen, boy, I brought you into this world; I can take you out."

But this commandment was not a threat; it was a promise. For the individual, the sound teachings of the parents — the good habits, the intelligent care of body and mind, the proper approach to spiritual things — would all tend to promise a longer and more productive life than if those early precepts were ignored. For society, proper honor to parents would serve as a good rule to maintain order and stability in the nation.

One thing should not be ignored: even though this commandment is particularly directed toward the responsibility of adult children, there is an equally important responsibility for parents to act in a way that allows the commandment to be faithfully kept. Honor is not automatic — in business, politics, religion, or even parenthood. Some parents, even good church folk, are atrocious, abusing their children physically and emotionally. Honor *that* mother or father? Mom, Dad, get your honor the "old-fashioned way" — *earn* it!

The apostle Paul writes, "Fathers, do not embitter your children, or they will become discouraged" (Colossians 3:21). Yes, children need discipline and parents ought to provide it. But Paul's message is to not do it so harshly that you break a child's spirit. Martin Luther, all his life, had a difficult time calling God "Father," not because of any pre-modern sensitivity to inclusive language, but because his own father had treated him so sternly while he was growing up. Luther could not identify the loving God that he had come to know in the scripture with what he knew of "father" in his own home. Support has to be a two-way street.

Honor to parents means respect, but respect is something that must be warranted. The obedience that parents get should not be the obedience that is given grudgingly to a dictator. It should come from a realization that what the parents ask is reasonable and, ultimately, for the child's good. It means a consistency of care and concern that begins in the child's infancy and continues forever. Parents should be respected, but they should respect their children enough to want to deserve it.

Parents need to remember one thing more to be worthy of the honor that the fifth commandment calls for. Parents must give their children a proper spiritual framework for life at an early age, or they may never hear that this commandment even exists. In the sacrament of baptism, we promise to raise our youngsters "in the knowledge and love of God." That means we take a vow to train them in God's precepts and to bring them up knowing the love

52

God has shown us in Jesus Christ. We promise to raise them in the church, and the church promises to help us do it. Christian children will be proud to honor mothers and fathers who fulfill those vows, moms and dads who talk the talk and walk the walk.

Every parent knows that children are a tremendous commitment. They change our lives. Children require real work, real dedication, real patience. But we know the real joy they can bring. And what a joy it will be to face our Lord one day and, seeing the godly lives of our children, be able to hear, "Well done."

"Family values" is a phrase often heard in our land these days. Sadly, it is most frequently used in an effort to deny basic rights to a certain segment of our community. But if we want to see how the truly just society that God intends for us understands family values, we simply reread this fifth commandment. "Honor your father and mother" — this is the commandment of God. And the nation that does that will find, "that you [will] live long in the land the Lord your God is giving you."

Study Questions

1. If this commandment is ancient Israel's "Social Security" legislation, how does that inform Social Security in our day?

2. How do we honor the elderly?

3. What happens when a society denigrates the elderly?

4. Social science insists that our past helps form us. What happens if we try to ignore it or pretend it is of no importance?

5. How can those who have been damaged by their family of origin overcome the hurt?

6. Think of some of the families we encounter in the Bible — what are the strengths and weaknesses we find?

1. See Exodus 21:15; Leviticus 19:3a; and Deuteronomy 27:6 for the penal code equivalent of this commandment.

Sixth Commandment

No Murder

Then God blessed Noah and his sons, saying to them, "Be fruitful and increase in number and fill the earth. The fear and dread of you will fall upon all the beasts of the earth and all the birds of the air, upon every creature that moves along the ground, and upon all the fish of the sea; they are given into your hands. Everything that lives and moves will be food for you. Just as I gave you the green plants, I now give you everything.

"But you must not eat meat that has its lifeblood still in it. And for your lifeblood I will surely demand an accounting. I will demand an accounting from every animal. And from each man, too, I will demand an accounting for the life of his fellow man. Whoever sheds the blood of man, by man shall his blood be shed; for in the image of God has God made man. As for you, be fruitful and increase in number; multiply on the earth and increase upon it." — Genesis 9:1-7

No murder! This is the word of the Lord ... and the word of the sheriff ... and the police chief ... and the governor ... and the president ... and mother — everybody! "You shall not murder" (and, by the way, "murder" *is* a more accurate translation of the commandment from the Hebrew than simply "kill" — the word means "violent, unauthorized" killing). We have no problem with that. No murder. It is illegal, immoral, and unjust. An easy commandment to understand ... and keep.

This commandment was initially given to prevent blood feuds — no Hatfields-and-McCoys-type vendettas in an eye-for-an-eye culture in which people's lives are at risk for no reason other than family ties. However, the "No Murder" commandment poses

55

additional questions. What about abortion? Is abortion murder, a violation of this sixth commandment? How about embryonic stem cell research? What about killing in war? Is that a violation of the commandment? What about capital punishment? Is the death penalty prohibited by "You shall not murder"? Or what about a terminally ill patient's appeal to Dr. Kevorkian to end a life of unending agony? Is it murder when someone compassionately helps put a person out of pain-filled misery? Not easy questions. We realize that human life is special, and we remember the commandment: "You shall not murder."

One thing should be made clear: We are saying *human* life is special in light of the command. Animal life, in spite of the fact that we might prefer that no harm come to helpless beasts, is not under consideration here. Genesis deals with that subject: God tells Noah after the flood, "Everything that lives and moves will be food for you." If we were not supposed to eat meat, God would have given us another kind of teeth, because what we have are designed to eat meat. "You shall not murder" means humans, not animals.

Are there certain circumstances where human beings can be killed? Abortion? War? Capital Punishment? Euthanasia? Much has been written on each of these ethical questions, and there is no way we could possibly get into all of the issues in the course of a short sermon (or even a very long one). But in connection with what the commandment says, we will consider them at least briefly.

What about abortion? Is it murder or not? Despite what some folks would have us believe, the scripture is *not* crystal clear on the issue. In Bible times, we have no record of any thought being given as to whether a pregnancy should be permitted to go to term or not; it just did. Within pagan societies, if an unwanted baby came along, the child was simply left to die or perhaps drowned. For the Jews, that would be an obvious violation of the commandment, so it was never practiced. The closest indication we get as to God's instruction on the matter concerns *accidental* killing. Perhaps there is guidance here concerning abortion.

If an Israelite accidentally killed someone, he was not automatically condemned. He could escape the wrath of the victim's family (who, by the eye-for-an-eye law, had the right to kill him) if

56

he could get to one of six "cities of refuge" that were strategically located throughout the nation. Upon presentation of his case, if the determination was made that the killing was indeed an accident and not premeditated, he would not be handed over to the victim's family for retribution. He could remain in the city in safety until the high priest currently ruling should die. After that, he would be free to go anywhere. He would have suffered a loss of liberty for a time, perhaps even a long time, but he was at least allowed to live.

But what about causing the death of an unborn child? Exodus 21:22 says, "If men who are fighting hit a pregnant woman and she has a miscarriage or premature birth, but there is no serious injury, the offender must be fined whatever the woman's husband demands and the court allows. But if there is serious injury, you are to take life for life." Is God making a distinction between the value of the born and the unborn? It sounds like it.

But there is another side. There are a number of references that indicate God's knowledge of us, even before we are born. For example, God told the prophet Jeremiah, "Before I formed you in the womb I knew you, before you were born I set you apart; I appointed you as a prophet to the nations" (Jeremiah 1:5). What would have happened had Jeremiah's mother had an abortion? I suspect God could have handled it, but how, I have no idea.

What, then, is the biblical position on abortion? Is it a violation of the sixth commandment? Some say, "Yes"; some say, "No." But a careful reading of the scripture leaves us not being able to say much of anything, so be careful about absolute pronouncements. We can base our arguments, either pro or con, on other factors, including personal preference, but the biblical evidence as to whether abortion is murder is not conclusive.

The position of the Presbyterian Church (USA) of which I am a part is that abortion is a wrenching choice, but it *is* a choice. In the case of rape or incest or if the mother's life is threatened, the church has said that abortion is a legitimate consideration. None of us would want to ruin the life of some helpless fourteen-year-old, pregnant as a result of rape. But we have also said that abortion is not legitimate as simply an after-the-fact method of birth control. And, in the case of so-called late-term abortion, the church has said that if the fetus is viable outside the womb, the preference is to save that baby. However, in terms of this present study, note that the arguments are based on considerations other than "You shall not murder."

A related issue: embryonic stem cell research. Sadly, this has become another political football, and the result is a setback for those hoping this ground-breaking work might soon result in cures for things like diabetes, Parkinson's disease, Alzheimer's, spinal cord injuries, and so on. The issue, as framed by those who oppose this work, is that these embryos are potentially human life, so research on them would be tantamount to murder. Those who favor the research point out that the vast majority of these stem cells will eventually be thrown out unused anyway; instead, we should put them to good use. Are these cells *life*? Folks continue to debate that. Some insist that life begins at conception, even if it is in a petri dish. For me, the operative scripture is Genesis 2:7 — "The Lord God formed the man from the dust of the ground and breathed into his nostrils the breath of life, and the man became a living being." Breath equals life. Once a fetus can breathe, we have a life. Until then, I would say, "No." From my theological perspective, to use these cells in research then would *not* violate this sixth commandment.

What about war? There are lots of stories about war in the Bible, a number even picturing God as commanding general. Does that mean that war is all right, a legitimate instrument of national purpose? Again, some say, "Yes"; some say, "No." The issue for us, of course, is whether or not war violates the sixth commandment because people are killed in war. If a soldier kills an enemy in battle, is he a murderer?

Some soldiers think so. Sometime back, on a millionth repeat of an episode of *M*A*S*H*, a wounded soldier was lying in the field hospital asking Father Mulcahy to please try to arrange for him not to be sent back to the front. The chaplain tried to comfort the young man by saying that he should not worry ... there was no shame in being afraid of injury, or even death — it was a perfectly normal reaction. But the soldier protested. It was not fear that concerned him — he had already killed three of the enemy in battle,

58

and he was afraid that if he were sent back, he would have to kill more, and he did not want to do it, enemy or not. He felt like a murderer.

Was he? The scripture does not say so. In Romans 13, Saint Paul goes on at some length about a citizen's responsibility to the state (vv. 1-7). He says that we are subject to the powers of the government. We are to obey our leaders when we are told to adhere to the civil law, to pay our taxes, and even when we are told to go to war.

One thing should be made clear, though: Paul had no intention of saying that we must obey the government even if the leadership is clearly operating contrary to the way God would have us live. With the benefit of 20/20 hindsight, the church knows that a Hitler should have been resisted. The same holds true for individual soldiers in the field. If a Christian is ordered by a commander to participate in a massacre such as occurred in Vietnam at My Lai or in Iraq at Haditha, the ethnic cleansing in eastern Europe, he or she would be compelled to resist on moral grounds. The slaughter of innocent noncombatants in wartime or any time can never be condoned, governing authorities notwithstanding. There are times when government must be resisted on moral grounds. To be sure, it might mean personal sacrifice for a soldier to refuse such a battlefield order — he or she could be subject to court martial and even execution. But there is no other ethical choice.

There are other questions concerning this sixth commandment. What about capital punishment? Again, the issue is complex. But we are not considering whether or not there should be such a thing, only are the judge who condemns a person to death and the one who is the actual executioner guilty of murder. Again, the scripture appears to say, "No."

Back to Genesis: "Whoever sheds the blood of man, by man shall his blood be shed; for in the image of God has God made man." All told, the Old Testament lists almost twenty crimes that were considered capital offenses — besides murder there were things like child sacrifice; perjury in a capital trial; keeping an ox that was known dangerous, especially after it had killed someone; kidnapping; insulting or injuring parents; sabbath breaking; and various forms of sexual immorality. In New Testament times, capital punishment was a well accepted method of dealing with criminals. Jesus never spoke against it, and as we know, he was its most famous victim.

Capital punishment is ordained by the state, and in some situations, not only permitted but required. Since that is the case, the Christian conscience need not be troubled about violation of the sixth commandment. Both judge and executioner are "subject to the governing authorities," as Romans 13 says. Christians may be troubled by the whole process and can legitimately object on moral grounds. I do. There are too many instances of the wrong person being convicted, and once the death penalty is meted out, it cannot be corrected if wrongly administered. I absolutely oppose capital punishment. But that is not the issue here. If the death sentence is passed, those who carry it out are not guilty of murder.

But what about a death sentence in which the state is *not* involved? Euthanasia, for example — mercy-killing — putting someone out of their misery who is suffering from an incurable disease? Or what about unhooking the miraculous machines that can keep us alive when our bodies are no longer able to manage? Terry Schiavo comes to mind. Does "You shall not murder" prohibit such things?

Many years ago, near the beginning of my ministry, I was called to the hospital to meet with the family of one of my parishioners who was very near death. He and his wife had decided some time before that, should the end come near, no heroic measures would be taken to prolong his life, no machines would do what his own body could no longer do. He would be allowed to die with dignity. But very early that morning he had stopped breathing and the doctors had reacted instinctively, the way they had been trained: They had put him on a respirator despite the previous agreement about no machines. I came into the hospital and the family immediately jumped me. What should they do? Would it be murder to tell the staff to unhook the machine? I asked them what they felt. They said they did not think so. I said neither did I (but I was not going to put them in the uncomfortable position of hearing that until they

60

were already comfortable with their own decision). The issue: Is allowing someone to die the same as killing? The answer: "No."

But what of the active help that some terminally ill patients request, the call to Dr. Kevorkian? Is it murder, a violation of this sixth commandment, to respond to the patient's pleadings? Civil authorities continue to wrestle with the question, and in this nation, only Oregon has an assisted-suicide law (since 1997) that permits physicians to administer lethal prescriptions. For the Christian, the word to love our neighbor puts us in a quandary here — we do not want people to suffer, and frankly, our faith tells us that death of the body is not the ultimate evil. But, painful though it may be, it is difficult to defend our own intervening where God has not chosen to do so.

Further problems arise in situations in which a patient is near the end of life, but is lingering ... and might linger in some sort of limbo between life and death for who knows how long. Existing, not living, no hope of recovery, and in the process draining everyone's emotional and financial resources. Should the process be "helped along"? After all, there would be reason to look askance at someone putting Grandpa peacefully to sleep who stands to inherit a million bucks once the old guy is gone. And we certainly would look askance at folks doing Gramps in just because they got tired of caring for him. For the Christian, the "love your neighbor" commandment jumps up again, but, once more, it is hard to justify direct intervention where God has chosen otherwise.

One more issue needs to be considered — suicide. Scientists tell us that the most overpowering instinct we have is that of self-preservation. If someone can deny that instinct long enough to take his or her own life, we could seriously question the rationality of the act. The sixth commandment was given to prevent blood feuds, not the taking of one's own life.

In the Sermon on the Mount, Jesus said that we can "murder" folks with angry insults (Matthew 5:22) — we disparage their worth as "images of God." In the twenty-first century he might say we do the same by failing to teach our kids properly about sex and letting them get to the place where abortion is a consideration; by failing to actively promote international justice without which war is an

61

ever-present danger; by allowing a society to exist where some folks feel they have to break the law and even kill simply to survive; by failing to provide the warmth of human love to those whose pain is so deep that death seems better than life. We may never have blown someone's head off, but this *is* a commandment we need to hear.

"You shall not murder." The issues are complex. On the one hand, the commandment was given to control society's baser instincts. But, on the other, it is a reminder that life is special. It is the word of a gracious and loving God who wants you to know that you are special. And God showed just how special by sending Jesus to die that we might live. In a world that rarely seems to care whether we live or die, that is good news indeed.

Study Questions

1. This appears to be a very straightforward prohibition — why, then, do we find a modern need to "parse" it and find exceptions everywhere?

2. What is the affirmative version of this commandment? Are we to defend the lives of our neighbors? Does that include taking up arms in their defense?

3. We find capital punishment in the Bible. Does that mean its continued use is justified?

4. Abortion remains a controversial issue in our society — should it be legal? If it remains legal, should there be limits as to when it can occur or the method used? Who should make these decisions?

5. The author suggests that the beginning of life can be marked once a fetus is able to breathe. Do you agree or disagree? Why?

Seventh Commandment

No Adultery

At dawn he appeared again in the temple courts, where all the people gathered around him, and he sat down to teach them. The teachers of the law and the Pharisees brought in a woman caught in adultery. They made her stand before the group and said to Jesus, "Teacher, this woman was caught in the act of adultery. In the Law Moses commanded us to stone such women. Now what do you say?" They were using this question as a trap, in order to have a basis for accusing him.

But Jesus bent down and started to write on the ground with his finger. When they kept on questioning him, he straightened up and said to them, "If any one of you is without sin, let him be the first to throw a stone at her." Again he stooped down and wrote on the ground.

At this, those who heard began to go away one at a time, the older ones first, until only Jesus was left, with the woman still standing there. Jesus straightened up and asked her, "Woman, where are they? Has no one condemned you?"

"No one, sir," she said.

"Then neither do I condemn you," Jesus declared. "Go now and leave your life of sin."   — John 8:2-11

I remember the first time I ever preached on this commandment. I was more than a little reluctant ... not because I was concerned about the sensitivity of the subject, but rather its relevance. You see, I was serving a congregation at that time that was *old*. I mean *really old* — 20% of them were over eighty! Did they *need* to hear, "You shall not commit adultery"?[1] But I was in the midst of a series on the Ten Commandments, so I could not comfortably

63

skip this one. I mentioned my concern, and the word that came back was, "This is the one we have been waiting for — just because there is snow on the roof does not mean there is no fire in the furnace."

On the other hand, how does one explain this to the children in church (presuming there happen to be any)? The reality is that we probably all would be either shocked or amazed at just how much our youngsters know, and particularly in light of everything they see and hear on television. How many parents had to explain to youngsters (or try to avoid explaining) what was going on after the Bill Clinton/Monica Lewinski debacle?

In a church I served years ago (in which there were lots of children), the five-, six- and seven-year-olds were studying about Moses, and they came to the story of the giving of the Ten Commandments. The teacher called the laws off one by one — the children explained what each one meant. Suddenly, they came to number seven: "You shall not commit adultery." The teacher gulped. What would these little ones know about adultery? And how would she explain it anyway? Sure enough, a couple of children raised their hands. One boy said something like, "It means when you're driving down the road, you're not supposed to look at the pretty women in the other cars." Another said, "It means that if a girl is wearing a dress, you're not supposed to look at her legs." Not bad answers, really. For children who would not possibly understand completely what this commandment is all about, they had somehow picked up on the relationship between sexuality and adultery.

Put yourself in the teacher's place. If the youngsters had not been able to come up with any answers, how would *you* have explained adultery? Of course, most folks do not bother to explain it; they figure kids will find out soon enough. True. Sex is something we all learn about — some sooner, some later.

There is the classic story of the father who wanted to make sure his eight-year-old son learned sooner rather than later, bought him a series of books on the subject, told him to read them, and then promised to answer any questions when he was done. The boy did the reading, then when the father asked for a reaction, the lad responded, "Well, it's all right if you like that sort of thing."

64

Of course, most everybody gets to the place where they *do* like that sort of thing. Sex is one of the most delightful gifts that God ever gave. Unfortunately, God's gift *can* sometimes create problems, and that is at least part of the reason we find this direction about "No Adultery."

To be accurate, when Moses came down from the mountain with this rule, it referred to a very specific sexual activity — that between a *married woman* and any man who was not her husband. A married man was guilty of adultery only in the case of having an affair with a *married* woman — nobody seemed to care if he slept with a prostitute. If it were a young, single lass, and sexual intercourse occurred, the man would have to marry the girl with no divorce ever allowed, a "life sentence" for both (Deuteronomy 22:29). It would not matter that the fellow might be already married and have a wife at home; polygamy was not a problem. Double standard? Absolutely. This is not a defense of that view, simply a stating of the facts as they existed.

Basically, the Jews looked upon adultery as a crime against property. A wife was the property of the husband; chances are he had paid her father for the privilege of marrying her. Remember the story of Jacob and Rachel and the fourteen years he had to work for her father Laban to get her? (Genesis 29:1-30). A husband had the right to expect that his wife belonged to him and him alone and that any children she might bear would be his. Adultery was not simply sexual sin.

Recall the fifth commandment: "Honor your father and mother," and the fact that the family was the basic building block of this new Israelite society. An insistence upon the care of elderly parents was the social security system. Now, this seventh commandment comes along — No Adultery. This one insures a just and decent society's orderly system of family survival through inheritance. If mother can be trusted to bring forth only children who are unquestionably the offspring of father, property will be passed from generation to generation without problems and it will *stay in the family* — bloodlines. But if mom fools around, who knows whose child might suddenly claim inheritance rights? The word "adultery" itself is instructive — it comes from a Latin root which means "to corrupt." When we talk about adulterated milk or soup, we mean that something has been introduced into it that makes it not as pure as it was. Adultery has the potential of introducing something "foreign" into the bloodline. Come inheritance time, this could get very confusing, not to mention incredibly nasty. No adultery! An instruction to keep folks morally pure? Only accidentally. This was designed to put one more protective fence around the family.

As we have noted before, the Ten Commandments are policy statements, more akin to our Bill of Rights than a penal code, but that does not mean that the prohibited behavior had no consequences in law. In the case of adultery in ancient Israel, the penalty was death. "If a man commits adultery with another man's wife — with the wife of his neighbor — both the adulterer and the adulteress must be put to death" (Leviticus 20:10). The method of death is not specified. In the case of a girl who is already engaged, both she and the man who seduced her are to be brought outside the city gates and stoned to death (Deuteronomy 22:24). The *Mishnah*, the Jewish law as expanded and explained by the rabbinical scholars, states that the penalty for adultery involving a married woman is strangulation — "The man is to be enclosed in manure up to his knees, and a soft towel set within a rough towel is to be placed around his neck (in order that no mark may be made, for the punishment is God's punishment). Then one man draws in one direction and another in the other direction, until he be dead."[2] Historically, it is safe to say that the penalty was rarely enforced, because as often as the commandment was violated, if we are to take the word of the prophets, there would have been dead bodies all over the place.

What became actual practice was divorce. If a wife or fiancée were found guilty of adultery, the husband threw her out. In the Christmas story, that is what Joseph figured to do with Mary (Matthew 1:18-25). If the husband were guilty of adultery, the wife's only choice was to beg him to take the necessary steps to free her. She could not initiate divorce proceedings on her own, because she had few rights in the eyes of the law. She was, after all, property, not much more than a slave.

The Christian understanding of the commandment became much more highly developed. With the words of Jesus as our guide, adultery came to be understood as *anything* that violates a marriage — not just Mom having intercourse with someone other than Dad, but even inordinate desire for someone else, and of course, that ultimate marriage violator, divorce. Women were no longer merely property; as Paul wrote, "Husbands ought to love their wives as their own bodies" (Ephesians 5:28), treated with the greatest possible care and concern. Casual sexual relationships came to be understood as just as immoral as those that defiled a marriage.

Without a great deal of change, that is the way most people think today — and that is why children would answer a question about the meaning of adultery with a description of anything having to do with an interest in the opposite sex. Folks still kick over the traces, of course, because sex is such a powerful drive and can cloud the judgment of the best of us. We excuse ourselves by saying that sex is a private matter — as long as nobody else gets hurt, we do not want anyone telling us what to do. And most of us do not want to tell anybody else ... unless they happen to be preachers (remember Jim Bakker or Jimmy Swaggert?) or politicians.

But is sex all that private? Ask the eighty-year-old grandmother who went to her doctor asking for birth control pills. The doctor looked at her rather strangely but went ahead and gave the prescription anyway. A few weeks later, she came in and reported that the pills were working wonderfully — she was sleeping like a baby.

"What?" the doctor asked. "Those are not sleeping pills; they keep ladies from getting pregnant."

"I know," said the grandmother. "Each morning I crush one up into my teenage granddaughter's orange juice, and I sleep like a baby!"

Sex is not simply a private matter. People *do* get hurt — the parents of an unwed mother, the children of divorce, the families of those who die from AIDS. A wonderful old episode of *Happy Days* has the father, Howard Cunningham, having to find a substitute bowling partner for an upcoming mixed doubles tournament because his wife had come down with a bad back. His new partner turned out to be quite a looker, and at the same time, one whom we might describe as of "easy virtue." She made no pretense ... she wanted him to come home with her and not just for coffee. Yes, he was tempted, but he turned her down flat. He said that he loved his wife and would never knowingly do anything to hurt her. The audience applauded. They knew he had done right. All of us know it. That is why we still call adultery a sin.

Of course, these days there is more at stake than simply a certain level of morality. Sleeping around can kill you. A cartoon has a young fellow saying to his grandfather, "Gee, Granddad, your generation didn't have all these social diseases. What did you wear to have safe sex?"

Grandfather replied, "A wedding ring."

One other subject must be addressed in connection with this seventh commandment ... divorce. Jesus said, "Anyone who divorces his wife and marries another woman commits adultery against her. And if she divorces her husband and marries another man, she commits adultery" (Mark 10:11-12). He seems to be saying that while a married person commits adultery by having sex with a single person, a single person — if divorced — could commit adultery by getting married.

No divorce ever? That would be wed*lock* with a vengeance! But what about the young girl who marries her boyfriend only to find out after the ceremony that he regularly flies into jealous rages and brutally beats her anytime he gets the notion? She divorces him to save herself from such terror, eventually marries a fine, loving man, makes a home with him, has children, is active in church and community, and they live happily ever after. Is she an adulteress? Or consider the strange innocence of a man who deserts his wife, disappears without a trace for years, is meanwhile divorced by his wife, finally comes back home to find her happily remarried, forces her to have sex with him, and then takes off again. The "no divorce ever" rule would mean that this would be okay. What do you think Jesus would say?

If we take as a given Jesus' concern for the welfare of people, we can get a clearer picture. Divorce was a serious social problem in the first century. A woman could be divorced for no other reason than that her husband was tired of her — she could be thrown out of the home with nothing more than the clothes on her back and no hope for keeping body and soul together except by prostitution or begging. No wonder Jesus would come down so hard on it. Sex was not the issue, survival was. A loving Lord could never condone such abuse.

Things are different now. Jesus would not call that young lady escaping the torture of an awful husband to find a decent life an adulteress. He would have called the long-lost husband who suddenly came back a rapist and a brute. I honestly think that if the question of divorce in situations like that were ever presented to the Lord, he would have helped those ladies file the papers.

Adultery is an often misunderstood issue ... and not only by young children. Probably the simplest way to explain it is to say that when men and women get married they make a promise that they will love each other in a way that they will never love anybody else, "as long as we both shall live." When one of them breaks that promise, that is adultery. The bad news is that lots of people *do* break the promise. The good news for those who have fallen is that there is real comfort — gospel — in one of the tenderest stories in all of scripture.

Poor woman! Dragged out of bed by a bunch of strange men. Maybe she had had time to wrap a sheet around her as she was led out of the house, maybe not. Paraded down the street, at least partially naked and then finally stopped in front of this wandering preacher. Now, they were asking about whether or not she should be stoned to death.

Why she did not faint from the terror of it all, we will never know. Maybe it was the gentleness in the attitude of the preacher as compared to the fierceness of her captors. Maybe it was the fact that he did not want to embarrass her any more than she already was, and instead of looking at her nakedness, he looked down at the ground and doodled in the dust.

When they asked him about killing her, he said, "Feel free, but only on condition that the one who throws the first stone has never been guilty of anything himself." Slowly, the crowd began to thin out. It had become apparent that the excitement was over for today. No stoning.

Finally, only the two of them were left there: the preacher and the woman. He asked what had happened to the crowd that wanted to kill her, and she said they had gone. She realized that he was looking at her now, but she was afraid to look at him. She turned her eyes to the ground, in shame. She knew that she had done wrong, and she was sorry. That was all he wanted. There was no scolding, no lecture about breaking the commandments, just two short sentences — to her and to us who perhaps have done much worse — two short sentences that give us faith in him and renew it in ourselves: "Neither do I condemn you. Go now and leave your life of sin."

Those who have ears, let them hear.

Study Questions

1. Our culture appears to have a horror of sexual sin of any kind — is our horror appropriate?

2. Adultery in the Bible involves some very specific parameters and is not simply a description of sexual intercourse between people who are not married. Is that how it is understood in our day?

3. What do you think of the biblical penalties for divorce cited in Leviticus and Deuteronomy? What penalties should exist today?

4. One of the most stunningly swift social changes in American society has been the almost universal acceptance of divorce where previous generations universally decried it. Is this a good thing or a bad thing?

5. The Bible routinely describes Israel's behavior in regard to God as "adulterous" — how is that to be understood?

1. See Leviticus 18:20; 20:10; Numbers 5:11-31; and Deuteronomy 22:22 for the penal code equivalent of this commandment.

2. Quoted by William Barclay, *The Daily Study Bible Series*, CD-ROM (Liguori, Missouri: Liguori Faithware, used by permission of Westminster/John Knox Press, 1996).

Eighth Commandment

No Stealing

If a man steals an ox or a sheep and slaughters it or sells it, he must pay back five head of cattle for the ox and four sheep for the sheep. If a thief is caught breaking in and is struck so that he dies, the defender is not guilty of bloodshed; but if it happens after sunrise, he is guilty of bloodshed. A thief must certainly make restitution, but if he has nothing, he must be sold to pay for his theft. If the stolen animal is found alive in his possession — whether ox or donkey or sheep — he must pay back double. — Exodus 22:1-4

Have you ever been robbed? Someone broke into your home or business or car or locker at school and took something? I have. A few years ago, someone broke into my car while it was parked on the street and took some things from the back seat. They were not expensive or irreplaceable, but it was a rotten feeling nonetheless. It was not so much that something I owned was stolen, but the feeling that part of *me* had been violated. There is a tie between us and our property that has nothing to do with the worth of a particular object, and the thought that someone would just *steal* part of *us* gives us the chills.

Jack and Mary Benny's New York hotel suite was once robbed and one of the things taken was his wife's most treasured piece, a magnificent diamond ring. Jack was in Pittsburgh at the time and only heard about what happened from a reporter. He phoned several times to get the details from Mary, only to be told on each occasion that she was out. When he finally got her, his first question was, "Where on earth have you been?"

"At the jeweler's," she said, "looking for another ring."

"What? At a time like this you're out looking for a diamond?"

"Sure," said Mary, "it's like falling off a horse. If you don't get right back on, you might never ride again."[1] Ha!

Unfortunately, burglaries occur all the time. If statistics are any guide, most of you have had something stolen. We read that one in four Americans will be a crime victim each year, and most of those crimes will be thefts.[2] Property crime occurs in this nation on average once every ten seconds.[3] The downtown church I served in Florida some years ago was regularly burglarized. There were muggings and purse snatchings (and even a murder) in the parking lot. Choir members were told to bring valuables with them into the choir loft during worship to protect them from being stolen from the choir room. Someone even came into the sanctuary and stole the cross from the communion table. It was a fun neighborhood.

It has been said that the only reason the stars are still in the heavens is that we cannot get our hands on them. There is more than a grain of truth in that. Independent retail studies have estimated theft from stores costs the American public more than $33-billion per year. Whole retail store chains have gone out of business due to their inability to control losses due to theft. And ultimately, of course, the cost of the losses are passed on to us, the consumers. It is estimated that shoplifting occurs upward of 440-million times a year. That equates to 1.2 million shoplifting incidents every day at a loss rate of between $19,000 and $25,300 stolen per minute.[4] Insurance companies say that 30% of all business failures each year are a direct result of internal theft: fraud, embezzlement, and similar crimes. Hotel managers say that one out of every three guests steals something.

These days, we face a new danger: identity theft. Shakespeare got it wrong when he said, "He that filches from me my good name/ Robs me of that which not enriches him/And makes me poor indeed."[5] Now we have nefarious folks who filch your good name very definitely with the idea of enriching themselves. You have "Dumpster Divers" who rummage through trash looking for bills or other papers with your personal information on it. You have people "Phishing" on the internet pretending to be financial institutions or online companies using deceit to get you to reveal your personal information. Some do it the old-fashioned way — they steal wallets and purses; mail, including bank and credit card statements; pre-approved credit offers; and new checks or tax information. They steal personnel records from their employers, or bribe employees who have access. It is a huge problem, and it is not getting better anytime soon.

Why? We all love the idea of getting something for nothing. Why do people spend so many millions in state lotteries around the country? Because folks want to support education and assistance to the elderly? Right. Something for nothing.

Of course, the problem is nothing new. When God said to the Israelites at Mount Sinai, "You shall not steal,"[6] there was nothing startling about the commandment. Theft had never been considered an acceptable way to acquire property. All the ancient codes of law in the nations that surrounded Israel spelled out penalties for thieves: in most cases, either mutilation or death.

The case law we find in Exodus 22 gives the penalties in the covenant community. Five oxen for a stolen ox, and four sheep for a stolen sheep, but only two for one if the originals are returned unharmed. If the thief is unable to make restitution, he "shall be sold for the theft" — a slave. Actually, rather lenient sentences compared to Israel's neighbors, except in the case of a nighttime cat burglar who literally took his life in his hands (he could be killed if caught in the act, and no one would have to answer for it). The Jews did not need to be reminded that burglary and highway robbery were not honorable professions. But they did need a reminder that God's standard for them, and for all generations, was honesty — honesty in all the ways we deal with one another, honesty in the way we respect other people's property.

A word here about property. Contrary to some egalitarian philosophies which make statements such as "Property is theft,"[7] the Bible sees nothing wrong with people owning things. If there were a problem with that, this commandment would have never been given. Right or wrong, *things* help to shape our identities — the clothes we wear, the cars we drive, the homes we live in, even Mary Livingstone's diamond ring, all say something to the world about who and what we are. To be sure, there are folks who go overboard in their conspicuous consumption, but simply because some do not handle property well is no reason to say therefore no one should own anything.

In general, good middle-class capitalist church types would agree with that. And, frankly, we might sit back and feel a little self-righteous about this one. We understand about ownership and private property. We have not robbed anybody lately. Oh? Well, maybe some office supplies or stamps from work, or even personal business conducted on the boss's time. It's wrong — and we know it. Fudging on the tax return — wrong — and we know it. Not repaying debts as we ought — wrong — and we know it. We are not guilty of armed hold-ups or muggings. We are talking about taking what rightfully belongs to another, regardless of how we do it, and we need this reminder.

Of course, come stewardship season each year, church people hear that familiar verse from Malachi, "Will a man rob God? Yet you rob me. But you ask, 'How do we rob you?' In tithes and offerings" (Malachi 3:8). That note is not to beat people up over their pledges or lack thereof but to call to mind just what the tithe and the various offerings were set apart for in the Israelite economy. Obviously, one of their purposes was for the maintenance of the temple and those who served there, just as it is today. But another use for the money given to the Lord was for the care and sustenance of those in the society who were unable to care for themselves. The covenant community realized that it had a responsibility in this regard, and they met it through the money they brought to the Lord.

The newspapers, with more regularity than we might like, have stories like this one.[8] Judy lives on welfare in the Watts section of Los Angeles with her two sons, Michael and Tiger. Every month, after she pays her bills she is about $25 light. There is always a lag between the time her money runs out and the food stamps come in. If the food stamps are late, she and the boys go hungry. They were a week late this time. She grew faint and vomited from hunger. Michael lay on the bed next to her and asked, "Mama, what are we gonna eat?"

"Suck your thumb and take a drink of water," Judy answered.

Michael sneaked into a neighbor's house, raided the kitchen, and came back with bacon and eggs. "Son," said Judy, "it's wrong to steal this stuff."

"Hell," Michael replied, "we got nothin' to eat."

Would you excuse something like that? If you would, you are not alone. The Bible says, "Thieves are not despised who steal only to satisfy their appetite when they are hungry" (Proverbs 6:30 NRSV). But note that stealing to feed yourself or your family is not glossed over; the penalty for someone who is caught is sevenfold restitution.

Still, it is not hard to relate to what Michael did. There is a terrible inequity between the "haves" and "have nots" in our society. Babies born into acute poverty are at the outset denied any realistic chance of "making it." But, in our heart of hearts, we also believe that God intends such children to have what is necessary for an abundant life. If they do not, whose fault is it? If they have been robbed of their future (and that does appear to be the best way to describe their predicament), who did the robbing? "Bad" people? They are robbed by power arrangements and structures that have long since relegated them to a permanent underclass. To those arrangements and structures, the command shouts out, "You shall not steal!"[9]

In this, the richest nation on earth, we would wish such situations would never occur. A few years ago, Alabama Governor Bob Riley, a conservative Republican and Southern Baptist, proposed a $1.2 billion tax package that would have raised taxes on the wealthiest residents and businesses and cut taxes on poor families. Riley argued that he had a moral obligation to do so. The governor's press secretary said, "Governor Riley has said many times that there are three things he has found in reading the New Testament: We are to love God, love our neighbor, and take care of the poorest of the poor."

In proposing the changes, Governor Riley noted that in Alabama, a family of four that made as little as $4,600 a year still had to pay income taxes. In neighboring Mississippi, that figure was $19,000. "I just don't think you can find a justification in the New Testament for taxing a family that makes $4,600 a year," he said.

The governor's tax plan passed the Alabama legislature but, when it faced a referendum of the voters, it went down to defeat, with the opposition led, ironically (or sinfully, if you like) by the conservative Christian Coalition.[10]

I continue to worry about the line in the Lord's Prayer we recite each week, the sentence that says, "Give us this day our daily bread." What concerns me is that that same line is prayed by millions of desperately poor and hungry people around the world. It is obvious that God has provided daily bread, and frankly, much more than we need. But it occurs to me that God is answering the prayer of those starving millions at precisely the same time and in precisely the same way as ours is being answered. In infinite wisdom, God is using us in a divine "warehousing" operation and giving us the responsibility to see that proper distribution is made. If that is the case, then we are some of the biggest thieves in history. We have been stealing the very life from countless suffering people around the globe by keeping so much of what we have in the "warehouse" for ourselves. If the force of the commandment "You shall not steal" is to remind us of the right of ownership and the necessity for basic honesty in dealing with things (even food), then "in all honesty," we had better realize that the right of ownership also belongs to those who own nothing. We have a responsibility to share.

Paul had something to say to the early church to which we need to pay attention: "Thieves must give up stealing; rather let them labor and work honestly with their own hands, so as to have something to share with the needy" (Ephesians 4:28). Some of those new Christians had apparently been highwaymen and burglars before coming to Christ; obviously, not an appropriate lifestyle for a disciple of Jesus. Paul does not say we are to stop stealing and work honestly so that we might support ourselves. He says stop stealing, and work honestly ... so that we might have something to *give*! After all, we cannot legitimately give something we have stolen, something that is not ours to give to begin with. I wonder what Paul would say to us. Perhaps the same thing. And not just to get us to keep our hands off what is not rightfully ours, but because a giving community — a generous community — is what ought to characterize Christ's church.

78

Throughout our study, we have been emphasizing that the Ten Commandments are, at their heart, God's way of putting together a just and decent society. The Decalogue is a social justice document. Obviously, when one person or entity wrongfully takes what belongs to another, that is unjust and ought not to happen. But a society that cares about *everyone's* property, including whether each one has enough, is the decent society, and unquestionably one that would gladden God's heart.

Are we there yet? Sadly, no. But one day, that blessed day when every knee will bow and every tongue confess that Jesus Christ is Lord — on *that* day, it will all come together.

Meanwhile, remember the word, all those who want something for nothing, those who would break into my car or your home or take Mary Livingstone's diamond ring, the identity thieves, those who filch from the office, who cheat on their taxes, who do not give a day's work for a day's pay, who do not pay their debts on time, and all of us who fail to properly share. Echoing down though the centuries, remember the word. "You shall not steal." Care about *everyone's* property, and be generous. It is a word we need to hear. It is a word we need to live.

Study Questions

1. Why do people who have been robbed feel violated?

2. Does our interest in getting a good deal, even paying less than an item is worth, fall into the category of theft?

3. Do you think God views someone who steals a candy bar from a grocery store in the same way as someone who is responsible for the loss of billions of dollars in retirement savings because of dishonest business practices? Why?

4. To what extent does our property define us?

5. Have you ever been the victim of identity theft? What happened?

1. Clifton Fadiman, Gen. Ed., *The Little, Brown Book of Anecdotes* (Boston: Little, Brown and Company, 1985), p. 55.

2. Albert Curry Winn, *A Christian Primer: The Prayer, the Creeds, the Commandments* (Louisville, Kentucky: Westminster/John Knox, 1990), p. 240.

3. John Holbert, *The Ten Commandments* (Nashville: Abingdon, 2002), p. 100.

4. http://www.crimedoctor.com/shoplifting-facts.htm.

5. William Shakespeare, *Othello*, Act iii, Scene 3 (New York: Penguin Group, 2001).

6. See Exodus 22:1-4 and Leviticus 19:11, 13 for the penal code equivalent to this commandment.

7. Pierre Joseph Proudhon, *What is Property?* (New York: Cambridge University Press, 1994).

8. Quoted by Lewis Smedes, *Mere Morality* (Grand Rapids, Michigan: Eerdmans, 1983), p. 202.

9. Walter Brueggemann, CD-ROM, "The Book of Exodus," *The New Interpreter's Bible*, Electronic Edition, Disk 3 (Nashville: Abingdon, 1997).

10. http://www.beliefnet.com/story/129/story_12980_1.html.

Ninth Commandment

No False Witness

If a malicious witness takes the stand to accuse a man of a crime, the two men involved in the dispute must stand in the presence of the Lord before the priests and the judges who are in office at the time. The judges must make a thorough investigation, and if the witness proves to be a liar, giving false testimony against his brother, then do to him as he intended to do to his brother. You must purge the evil from among you. The rest of the people will hear of this and be afraid, and never again will such an evil thing be done among you. Show no pity: life for life, eye for eye, tooth for tooth, hand for hand, foot for foot. — Deuteronomy 19:16-21

"The truth, the whole truth, and nothing but the truth, so help me God." Everyone is familiar with those words, and they come from the same milieu as this commandment. "You shall not bear false witness against your neighbor." If the Ten Commandments are, at heart, a social justice document designed to lay out God's basis for a just and decent society, and if that just and decent society is to have a mechanism for settling inevitable disputes — a court system — then these words about truthful testimony are the foundation.

We dislike perjury. People who swear to tell the truth but then lie give us a queasy feeling. One might want to say that it depends upon what someone is lying about as to the seriousness of the offense, but, nonetheless, the truth is preferable, and has always been. As one commentator has written, "Primitive men who killed and raped and looted without a second thought regarded a false oath as an offense against the gods, and looked with superstitious horror for a bolt of lightning to strike the blasphemer dead."[1]

Of course, the prohibition against false testimony in court was not unique to the Jews. Three hundred years before the Ten Commandments, Hammurabi's code said the same. That went so far as to lay out the sentence for those who were convicted of lying in court: one so convicted would have to bear the same penalty as the one who had been originally charged would have borne. For example, if someone perjured himself in a capital trial (where the penalty was death), then the one judged guilty of giving the false testimony was himself sentenced to die. One would surmise that such stiff punishment would have tended to be a good deterrent.

When it became part of the Jewish code of conduct in Deuteronomy 19, the same penalty was laid out.[2] But there were even prohibitions attached to the code to prevent people from being tempted to lie in court. Some were not even allowed to testify because they might consider perjuring themselves: relatives, friends, known enemies, anyone whose profession was thought of as in the least disreputable (dice-players, usurers, or slaves). The Jewish legal system was designed to protect the rights of the accused at every turn. Circumstantial evidence was not permitted. So, most certainly, fabricated verbal evidence was despised.

This commandment prohibiting false witness was first and foremost forensic in nature. Its prime focus was testimony before a court. The reason it did not flatly prohibit lying of any sort is that these Ten Commandments are not to be understood as a code of personal conduct. The concern here is justice, for a society that would protect the weak from the strong, the poor from the rich, the simple from the crafty. The opposite side of that coin called for an active defense of those who had been slandered, those who were in the dock because of lies, rumors, or innuendo. As the Jewish law laid it down, "If a person sins because he does not speak up when he hears a public charge to testify regarding something he has seen or learned about, he will be held responsible" (Leviticus 5:1). "False witness" could be given, not just by opening your mouth, but by keeping it shut as well. There is a bias toward truth in assuring a society that is as God intends, not only in this ninth commandment and the rest of the Jewish law, but throughout history.

As to personal truthfulness (not simply judicial), we learn early on. One of the first Bible verses my parents taught me was "Lying lips are an abomination to the Lord" (Proverbs 12:22). And every time I would be tempted to skirt the truth, I would see a wagging finger and hear, "Lying lips...." It's nothing new — the standard for proper conduct is a strict adherence to the truth. George Washington and the cherry tree and all that.

As to the way folks actually handle truth, though, that cherry tree story is wonderful. It first appeared in Parson Weems' biography, *Life of Washington*, in the 1806 edition. According to Weems' story, young George was given a hatchet at about the age of six and went around his daddy's farm testing his present out on all sorts of things, including a young cherry tree which was damaged severely. Papa summoned the boy and asked if he knew anything about it, and got the response, "Father, I cannot tell a lie; I cut the cherry tree." Because George was so truthful, his daddy forgot his anger, and all lived happily ever after. We have all heard that story. It has had an enormous effect on the kids of every subsequent American generation and has succeeded in making George Washington the sworn enemy of all young children.[3] It certainly has not made them more truthful. Ironically, this story about the virtue of telling the truth is itself not true — Parson Weems or somebody made it up. *O tempora, O mores.*

I wish I could say that preachers were innocent of that sort of thing. There is the classic story of the young boy coming home on a Sunday afternoon and asking his minister father about something he heard in the morning's sermon. "Daddy, was that really true, or was it just preachin'?"

What is surely true is that many times we do not think of what we say as lying, whether it be about George and the cherry tree or some quirky little invention for a sermon. But if what we pass on to someone else is less than the whole truth and we do not make that clear, what comes out of our mouth most certainly qualifies as a lie. Worst of all, lots of the lies we tell are not even for our own advantage, so we do not think of them as lies. They are just conversation. We call it gossip, and that can be deadly.

The Salem Witch Trials are instructive. In the summer and fall of 1692, over a hundred people were arrested and convicted for being "in league with the Devil." The only way they could escape the hangman's noose was to confess their awful crime and be granted mercy by the court. Twenty of them refused to confess to something of which they were not guilty and were legally murdered. How could such a thing have happened? Because the ridiculous gossip of some teenage girls got out of hand. In this case, lying lips were an abomination, not only to the Lord, but to the history of civilization.

It would be wonderful to say that such goings on were limited to the unsophisticates of the seventeenth century, but it was repeated in the early 1950s with the Army-McCarthy hearings, the House Unamerican Activities Committee, and the Hollywood Black Lists. In a generation that had just been at war twice within five years, there was genuine terror of anything that could threaten us again. The fear of the "Red Menace" was so gripping that anyone even whispered about as being sympathetic to Communism was in danger of having life and career flushed right down the drain. Many had that happen, and all because of the same kind of gossip that the girls of Salem had spread so many years before. It was wretched excess, of course, and Arthur Miller used the Salem Witch Trial experience as a parable to attack McCarthyism in his wonderful play, *The Crucible*.

"You shall not bear false witness against your neighbor." Good words for the courtroom, good words for *any* room. It is *not* a flat prohibition against lying. It would have nothing to say to me if I lied to protect someone. If a man came to me wielding a machete, asking if I had seen his wife, threatening to chop her up into fish bait when he finds her, I would surely tell him that I had not laid eyes on her, despite the fact that she was at that moment hiding in my closet. If the gestapo had come to my door looking for Jews to ship off to the concentration camp, I would have surely lied to protect the Goldberg family cowering in my attic. If a mother hands me her ugly little baby and asks if he is the cutest little boy I have ever seen, I am not going to tell her, "No, he looks like a young prune." If the reason God gave this commandment in the first place was to insure that people would not be wounded by words, you can know that God would never countenance wounding as the price for absolute truth.

One other issue in regard to this commandment: it comes from the *Larger Catechism* developed in conjunction with the venerable Westminster Confession of Faith. This from the section on how we are to understand the Ten Commandments:

> *Q. 145. What are the sins forbidden in the Ninth Commandment?*
>
> *A. The sins forbidden in the Ninth Commandment are: all prejudicing of the truth, and the good name of our neighbors as well as our own, especially in public judicature; giving false evidence, suborning false witnesses, wittingly appearing and pleading for an evil cause, outfacing and overbearing the truth; passing unjust sentence, calling evil good, and good evil; rewarding the wicked according to the work of the righteous, and the righteous according to the work of the wicked; forgery, concealing the truth, undue silence in a just cause, and holding our peace when iniquity calleth for either a reproof from ourselves, or complaint to others....*[4]

And then on and on some more. The phrase "undue silence in a just cause" jumps out. If the establishment of a fair and impartial judicial system for this newly freed nation of Israel is God's mind and motivation for giving this commandment, that will mean more than insuring against perjured testimony.

Consider one facet. True justice means appropriate sentencing, as the Catechism suggests, and unfortunately, in American jurisprudence in our day, that can be problematic. The difficulty is the result of public concern that too many criminals are walking our streets free because of legal technicalities or lenient judges. Politicians have seized on that and passed draconian "sentencing guidelines" that tell judges what sentences must be imposed for particular crimes — the "judgment" is no longer the prerogative of the judge. The result has been that, occasionally, someone is convicted and sentenced to a punishment that does not nearly fit the crime.

The most notorious of these situations occurs in states with a so-called "Three Strikes" law. These are statutes which require state courts to hand down a mandatory and extended period of incarceration to persons who have been convicted of a serious criminal offense on three or more separate occasions. The practice is not new. New York State, for example, has had a "persistent felony offender" law that dates back to the late nineteenth century, but sentences were not compulsory in every single case, and judges had much more discretion as to what term of incarceration should be imposed.

The first true "three strikes" law, with virtually no exceptions provided, was not enacted until 1993, when Washington state voters approved it. California followed a year later, when that state's voters approved "Proposition 184" by an almost four-to-one margin. The concept swiftly spread to other states and by 2004, 26 states and the federal government had "three strikes" statutes on the books (although none were quite so strong as California's). Some states require all three felony convictions to be for violent crimes if the mandatory sentence is to be pronounced, while others — most notably California — prescribe it for any third felony conviction so long as the first two felonies were deemed to be either "violent" or "serious," or both.

Some unusual scenarios have arisen, particularly in the Golden State. California punishes shoplifting and similar crimes as felony petty theft if the person who committed the crime has a prior conviction for any form of theft, including robbery or burglary. As a result, some defendants have been given sentences of 25-years-to-life in prison for such crimes as shoplifting golf clubs, videotapes, or even a slice of pepperoni pizza. In one particularly notorious case, Kevin Weber was sentenced to 26 years to life for the crime of stealing four chocolate chip cookies.[5] As you can imagine, sentences like this have prompted some criticism.

During the time I served a congregation in North Carolina, we heard about a young man named Kwame Cannon,[6] a young African-American man who, in 1986, as a seventeen-year-old, committed and was convicted of six "cat burglaries." He broke into people's homes while they were sleeping, never with a weapon, never injured anyone, and, in total, stole less than $500 worth of goods. His sentence? Two consecutive *life* terms!

One year before Kwame's sentencing, his mother had played a major role in a successful $300,000 lawsuit in which Greensboro Police, the Ku Klux Klan, and American Nazis were found liable in the wrongful deaths of five protesters in what became known as the 1979 Greensboro Massacre. Mrs. Cannon was well known as a social activist on issues pertaining to poor people and African Americans. Whether or not her son's sentence was at all related to that fact is only surmise.

Two consecutive life terms was the harshest sentence for comparable crimes in the history of North Carolina. Kwame Cannon committed crimes and deserved to be held accountable, as he himself willingly admitted. He publicly apologized for his burglaries. Kwame was a model prisoner. He made the effort to rehabilitate himself, took correspondence courses, studied to take the SAT (and one of his burglary victims served as his tutor). He served as "counselor" to other prisoners. He was praised by prison officials, ministers, political officials, and virtually everyone who saw this young man turn himself around.

Simple justice demanded that something be done to overturn the outrageously excessive sentence. Over 5,000 letters were written to North Carolina's Governor Jim Hunt requesting Kwame's release. The majority of the Greensboro City Council, including the mayor, requested his release. A former state supreme court justice and congressman, the 100-plus members of the Greensboro Pulpit Forum, as well as hundreds of people from all walks of life in Greensboro, asked that this young man be freed. Even the district attorney and the Greensboro chief of police said they did not oppose the release of Kwame Cannon.

In spite of all this, Governor Hunt did not appear to want to respond. If this ninth commandment demands not only an adherence to truthful testimony in our administration of justice, but as the Catechism insists, is a prohibition against "undue silence in a just cause," something had to be said. People spoke ... and spoke and spoke and spoke. Finally, a year later, the Governor signed the release and Kwame Cannon came home.

God cares about justice. That is the message, not only of the Ten Commandments, but of the entire corpus of scripture. God's aim is a society where there is fairness and equity for all, where judicial decisions are based on truth, where gossip has no place, where the sentence fits the crime, and where voices do not remain silent while injustice is done. To help us along that road, God gave us these good words, words to live and live well by: "You shall not bear false witness against your neighbor."

Study Questions

1. Is it possible for a complex society to exist without a court system? Why or why not?

2. If a court system is deemed necessary, what safeguards are needed to insure its fairness?

3. How do you feel about "sentencing guidelines" for judges?

4. Does it matter whether people take an oath to tell the truth in court? Are those who swear to tell the truth more truthful than those who do not?

5. What instances of "undue silence in a just cause" can you think of?

6. People lie. Why?

---

1. Joy Davidman, *Smoke on the Mountain* (Philadelphia: Westminster Press, 1954), p. 107.

2. See Exodus 23:1 and Deuteronomy 19:16-21 for the penal code equivalent to this commandment.

3. Clifton Fadiman, Gen. Ed., *The Little, Brown Book of Anecdotes* (Boston: Little, Brown and Co., 1985), p. 571.

4. *The Constitution of the Presbyterian Church (USA), Part I, Book of Confessions* (Louisville, Kentucky: Geneva Press, 1996), 7.257.

5. http://en.wikipedia.org/wiki/Three_strikes_law.

6. *The Prism*, via Internet, http://www.sunsite.unc.edu/prism/apr98/seventy.html.

No Covetousness

No one can serve two masters. Either he will hate the one and love the other, or he will be devoted to the one and despise the other. You cannot serve both God and Money.

Therefore I tell you, do not worry about your life, what you will eat or drink; or about your body, what you will wear. Is not life more important than food, and the body more important than clothes? Look at the birds of the air; they do not sow or reap or store away in barns, and yet your heavenly Father feeds them. Are you not much more valuable than they? Who of you by worrying can add a single hour to his life?

And why do you worry about clothes? See how the lilies of the field grow. They do not labor or spin. Yet I tell you that not even Solomon in all his splendor was dressed like one of these. If that is how God clothes the grass of the field, which is here today and tomorrow is thrown into the fire, will he not much more clothe you, O you of little faith?

So do not worry, saying, "What shall we eat?" or "What shall we drink?" or "What shall we wear?" For the pagans run after all these things, and your heavenly Father knows that you need them. But seek first his kingdom and his righteousness, and all these things will be given to you as well. — Matthew 6:24-33

Will Rogers once told of being approached by someone in a great state of excitement claiming that an enemy submarine had invaded one of our harbors; the man was wanting to know how the country could get rid of it. Will thought for a minute and said, "That's easy, boil the water in the harbor."

But the questioner persisted. "That's a great idea, but how do we do that?"

Rogers responded, "Hey, I am a concept man. You will have to work out the details for yourself."

Suddenly, we are confronted with "You shall not covet." For a capitalist society which has built itself into one of the most powerful economic forces on earth by setting our sights high, by creating in us a desire, a covetousness, for more and better of almost everything, these are hard words to hear. The concept is fine, but, as the old phrase goes, "the devil is in the details." How do we boil the water?

At first blush, this sounds like a strange commandment. Why on earth would God tell us not to want things? And frankly, how could a normal person keep from wanting things? Does it make sense for God to tell an African mother not to want food for her starving baby? Does it make sense for God to tell a man living in a cardboard box under a railroad bridge not to want a decent home? Does it make sense to tell parents not to want the wherewithal to provide an education for their children? On the face of it, "You shall not covet" is more than strange; it is nonsense.

The problem comes when we render this commandment simply as "You shall not covet." Leaving it at just those four words is an incomplete reading and can lead to misunderstanding. Leaving it there and ignoring the context can also lead to misunderstanding.

Reverse order. First, the context. During the study of the other commandments we have noted that God's aim in giving these rules was the creation of a just and decent society, one in which all are treated fairly and honestly. They are "policy statements," tantamount to the Bill of Rights in the US Constitution, not so much guidelines for specific action, but a framework from which those specifics might be formed. The first two commandments — it is unjust to delude people into pursuing false gods, whether ancient pagan deities or their modern equivalents (money, power, pleasure, and the like) that ultimately demean and destroy. The third commandment — it is unjust to treat people dishonestly by not being as good as your word. The fourth commandment — it is unjust to overwork people (even yourself). The fifth commandment — it is unjust to allow aging parents (or anyone else who might be vulnerable) to go without the necessities of life. Number six — it is unjust to pursue blood feuds and kill. Number seven — it is unjust to put a man's home and family at risk, to jeopardize inheritance rights, by seducing his wife. Eight — it is unjust to take someone's private property without permission. Nine — it is unjust to subvert the judicial system with false testimony or anything else. Justice is the trumpet that sounds through every commandment. The obvious conclusion, of course, is that this word against covetousness would follow that same pattern.

The other problem is the incomplete reading. The commandment is often quoted as "You shall not covet," and left at that. It says more. Specifics are mentioned: house, wife, male or female slaves, ox, donkey, property in general. The prohibition is not all-inclusive. It does not say that we are not to want food for our babies, a decent home for ourselves, or the money to pay for school for our kids. It is fine and even noble to want all that, but it is *not* fine, and certainly *not* noble, to set our hearts on what rightfully belongs to someone else.

The rationale is simple if we take the context seriously. If this is part of a document dealing with issues of social justice, the conclusion must be that wanting what belongs to our neighbor leads to injustice. And an unjust social order is contrary to the will of God.

A word here about justice. Very often, like beauty, justice is in the eye of the beholder. To a grocer, it is unjust that someone should steal a loaf of bread, but to the father who stole it, it is unjust to let his child starve. To an employer, it may seem unjust to be forced to pay a worker a certain minimum wage regardless of the task performed, but to the employee, forty hours of labor to only collect enough at the end of the week to support a family at the poverty line is also unjust. To a banker, it is unjust when folks do not repay their honest debts, but to the one about to be evicted in a foreclosure proceeding, it is seen as unjust to be tossed out in the street. What is just and what is unjust depend upon one's point of view.

Some years ago, a seminar on Christian faith and economics was held at Presbyterian College in Clinton, South Carolina. The day began with a lecture by Dr. Douglas Oldenburg, at the time the president of Columbia Theological Seminary (and eventually elected as Moderator of the General Assembly of the Presbyterian Church [USA]), who had recently completed a sabbatical during which he had done extensive study of economic issues in light of scripture and faith. The lecture was titled, "A Biblical Vision of Economic Justice." Dr. Oldenburg defined justice as "giving what is due." Unfortunately, as has already been noted, people disagree on "what is due" — how to boil the water in the harbor — so any help in that area would be most appreciated.

Dr. Oldenburg gave three principles for making that determination. First, people are due what they deserve — folks ought to get what they earn and earn what they get. Basic fairness; most would agree with that. But biblical justice does not stop there, so there is a second principle: people are due some things because of their worth as human beings — equal protection under the law, the right to vote, and so on. Again, basic fairness, and most can go along with that. Finally, the third principle: people are due what they *need* regardless of merit. Most would agree that even the worst of us cannot simply be left to starve in the street; that a criminal should not be denied medical attention even if wounded while committing the crime. Good, solid biblical principles to insure the kind of society God would establish.

Which of those principles takes precedence when they come into conflict though? For example, does my right to my hard-earned income take precedence over my neighbor's right to food? There is no easy answer, but perhaps this tenth commandment can offer guidelines.

Consider the items listed. "You shall not covet your neighbor's house." What would make that unjust? Can we not dream of getting as fine a home as the Joneses down the street? Of course, we can. What it means is that we have no right to earnestly desire (which is the definition of the word covet) ... to *earnestly desire* the Joneses' house itself because the temptation will be there to find some way to get it (and that is the force of the Hebrew word *chamad* in the commandment), whether the Joneses want to keep it or not. The further danger is that, if we do get the Joneses' house, the

Joneses might not have one, and, if the commandment is our guide, to let someone become homeless is unjust.

Does this mean that there should be no real estate business, that no property should ever change hands except by inheritance? Not at all. Buying and selling property was just as much a part of the Israelite economy as it is our own. But there was one major difference: Hebrew law tried to insure that, should a father find it necessary to trade or sell the family farm, the children and grandchildren would not be permanently condemned to a landless underclass. The rule was that every fiftieth year, the year of jubilee, all property would automatically revert to the family of original ownership — slaves were to be freed, land was to be returned (Leviticus 25:8 ff). Debts were to be canceled every seventh year (Deuteronomy 15:1). People would regularly have the chance to start with a clean slate. In that way, no real or imagined injustice would be perpetuated.

How about "You shall not covet your neighbor's wife"? Seducing her is already forbidden in the seventh commandment, but there is a further step than a "one night stand" implied here. Sex is not the issue, property is. Granted, men no longer consider wives as property (not if we want to stay alive), but ancient Israel did have that understanding, and with that in mind, the rule here is do not set your heart on having something of someone else's that would unjustly upset the basic unit of society that insures the provision of the necessities of life, the family.

There was good reason for such a rule. It had nothing to do with any emotional trauma that a family break-up might cause. It was economics. In Hebrew society, it was a man's right to have a family because children insured that the parents would be cared for in their old age. As was noted in studying the fifth commandment, the family was the Israelite answer to Social Security.

"You shall not covet your neighbor's male or female slave, or ox, or donkey...." Again, the issue is property, but in this case, the special property that allows someone to create a sustainable existence. In other words, it would be unjust for you to want those things of your neighbor's that help him make a living. The farmer had a right to his plow, the carpenter had a right to his hammer, and so on.

Other ancient laws even sought to insure that those who, for one reason or another, did not have property of their own, would still be able to survive. The rule about gleaning made sure that some grain around the edges of every field and some grapes in every vineyard would be left for the poor of the community to gather and sustain themselves (Leviticus 19:9-10). To be sure, those gleanings were not just handed out; that poor person had to come and do the gathering, but the foundation of the law was an understanding that people had an inherent right to make a living.

Finally, the catchall, "You shall not covet *anything* that is your neighbor's." If there is anything that belongs to someone else that, in your heart of hearts, you would like to take for yourself, do not even think about it. The temptation to stoop to injustice in satisfying that desire is too great to fool with.

Justice, justice, justice ... giving someone what is due. The commandment *is* helpful. Apparently, God's standard for a just society involves a home, a family, and the chance to make a living. And when Dr. Oldenburg's three principles of justice come into conflict with one another, these standards can be applied to sort out any difficulties.

First, the right to a home. According to the commandment, it is unjust for people to sleep over heating grates on our city streets. It is unjust for a society to care nothing about citizens who have never had and probably never will have enough money to buy a home.

Second, the right to family. According to the commandment, it was unjust to create welfare rules in times past that demanded that a household not have an able-bodied father living in the home to qualify for public assistance. Thousands of fathers had to leave wife and children just to allow the mother and babies to qualify for government help.

Third, the right to a decent lifestyle. According to the commandment, it is unjust to be satisfied with unemployment. It is unjust to leave some workers behind in a changing economy simply because of lack of training. It is unjust for mills and factories to be shut down and loyal employees thrown out in the street just because some corporate "down-sizer" decides to maximize profits. It is unjust to pay millions of tax dollars to store grain and cheese and milk when citizens are forced to rely on food banks and soup kitchens to supplement their diets. It is unjust to pay farmers *not* to plant crops when hundreds of millions of people around the world — hundreds of millions for whom Christ died — are living in abject poverty and 30,000 infants die *daily* because of improper nutrition.

Why do such injustices exist? Not because of lack of resources. Oldenburg noted that, according to the World Bank, it would take a redistribution of only two percent of the global food supply, only 2%, to wipe out malnutrition on this planet. Unfortunately, some folks have taken and kept for themselves what, according to this commandment, rightfully belongs to others. Why? Is it meanness — selfishness — greed? Some of that perhaps, but more likely it is just the normal concern that we keep our *own* home, our *own* family, and our *own* decent life. We do not want any children to go hungry, but most of all, not our *own*.

Such thinking has been around since the beginning of history. Centuries ago, on a gentle Judean hillside, Jesus talked about it. He said, "Do not worry about things like that. Your heavenly Father knows what you need. God takes care of the birds of the air and flowers of the field. Are you not worth more than they?"

These are difficult issues, no question, and generally beyond the scope of decent individuals to solve. But frankly, whether or not a mother has food enough to feed her baby should have nothing to do with how many decent individuals are around. Firm public policies and legislation should be in force to see that *all* citizens have a chance for their due — a home, family, and an opportunity for a decent life. The task of the church and all people of faith is to insist that society address these questions, and further, to challenge our elected officials with our lobbies and our votes and our willingness to participate in the electoral process to see that justice is done.

Some years ago, Henry Kissinger, the former secretary of state, and William Sloane Coffin, at the time the minister of Riverside Church in New York City, were on television together. The Vietnam War was the topic, but the conversation could have just as easily been in the context of those injustices that have been mentioned here. In exasperation, Dr. Kissinger asked, "But what would you have us *do*?"

Coffin responded, "As a minister, it is my task to say 'let justice roll down like waters, and righteousness like an ever flowing stream.' It is *your* job to design the irrigation system."

"You shall not covet" — and in particular the things that are the *due* of your neighbor — for the good of society, is at least as good a concept as boiling the water in the harbor. When the commandment is taken seriously, when we begin to get to the details, that is the beginning of justice. For those who are serious, we do well to remember what Jesus said on that hillside: "Seek first for the kingdom of God and [God's] righteousness, and all these things will be given to you as well."

Study Questions

1. Is it possible to legislate desire?

2. According to this commandment, what should be the limits of our ambition?

3. How does wanting things destroy community? What does it lead us to do?

4. Can pursuing things we want be a good thing? For example, if the pursuit makes us work harder?

5. What do you make of the way some traditions divide this into two commandments rather than one? Does that help or hurt our understanding?

www.ingramcontent.com/pod-product-compliance
Lightning Source LLC
Chambersburg PA
CBHW072008060426

42446CB00042B/2245